MODERNISM
A RECORD AND REVIEW

MODERNISM

A RECORD AND REVIEW

By

A. LESLIE LILLEY

Vicar of St. Mary's, Paddington

KENNIKAT PRESS
Port Washington, N. Y./London

MODERNISM

First published in 1908
Reissued in 1970 by Kennikat Press
Library of Congress Catalog Card No: 75-102575
SBN 8046-0735-4

Manufactured by Taylor Publishing Company   Dallas, Texas

TO

MY DEAR FRIEND AND FELLOW-COUNTRYMAN

GEORGE TYRRELL

EPISTLE DEDICATORY

My dear Tyrrell,

These pages seek the grace of an imputed merit in offering themselves as an act of homage to the lustre of your name. They are but an incomplete and haphazard record of a movement whereof you have been a great part. You and your friends have written an inspired and inspiring page in the history of religious thought. I have but scribbled some stray notes on its margin. It is in the hope that these collected notes may avail to send many to a study of the original documents that I now venture to publish them. Their purpose will secure for them your acceptance and approval, how far soever their actual accomplishment may be from deserving either. And here, fortunately, for once, value consists even more in purpose than in accomplishment.

Nor will it be an occasion of reproach against me on your part if I have addressed these papers primarily to what I conceive to be the needs and the opportunities of my own Communion. For that Communion was once yours also. You went out from among us in the days of your boyhood, days which you had already dedicated to that determined and courageous quest of truth which you have never abandoned. You went out from your own people, even from your own country, from relatives and friends who had so eagerly hoped to see your unquestioned ability developed in the service of the Church of your baptism, from the University which so many men of your name and family had illustrated, and which you in your turn might eventually have no less adorned, from the religious traditions, habits, prejudices of three centuries. You went out to seek in the Church of Rome the friendship of all the saints of God, to enrol yourself in that ancient University which meets in every Roman school about the feet of the Angelic Doctor, to live through a more venerable and inclusive tradition and to escape if it might be the warping effects of a narrow and exclusive prejudice. And you have found no cause to regret that spiritual adventure of your boyhood. For through Rome you have learned the lore of the saints and translated it for us into the universal language of religion. Through Rome you discovered your intellectual kinship with the mystics for whom the undeniable religious miracle was given in their own immediate experience, in their inner sense of God. Through Rome, too, you learned that analogical value of religious terms which you have so courageously and skilfully applied to the defence and illustration of the faith. And through Rome you still look on to that Catholic Church which will have inherited the divine beatitude by claiming as its own all who anywhere are hungering and thirsting after righteousness.

Nor have you for a moment thought it necessary or even possible to abandon the Church of your deliberate adoption, even when quite recently you heard the voice of authority raised against you in formal condemnation. You know too well the nature of a Church and the nature and limits of authority in a Church. For you a Church is

a spiritual fatherland, your due allegiance to which no
authority can in the last resort either assess or guarantee.
Authority indeed is essential, but it discharges its special
function only when it waits upon life and ministers to it.
When it attempts to prescribe to life the limits within
which it must move and beyond which it must not
venture, it has ceased to be ministrant to life and is engaged, whether it knows it or not, in preparing death.
Then it becomes a duty to resist it in its own interests,
to resist it in order that it may renew its character and
methods and become once again an authentic force of
direction and control. The limits of the coercive power
which it may legitimately exercise are prescribed for it
by the verdict of life as to what things have proved in
general and continuous experience to be morally hurtful.
Yet these are just the things on which authority (perhaps
wisely, for even here there may be some shrunken and
distorted growth of life) has always borne most lightly ;
while with the obstinate blindness which has characterised
it at many a moment of its history it crushes the forces
which would renew life and open out to it the way of
progress. Authority through those who have wielded it
has too often identified itself with its accidental and
temporary forms. At such times it is necessary for it to
learn that its forms are of the things that can be shaken
and must be shaken in order that the things which cannot
be shaken, life and the authority which proceeds from it,
may remain. The rulers of every spiritual society need
to learn from secular history the lesson that the best
citizens of the temporal fatherland have often been those
who resisted even to the death the unlimited claims of

some temporary form of authority arrogating to itself that divine right which was even then, through the changing needs and conditions of life, passing to another form. Both in the temporal and the spiritual spheres authority proves its divine right by being limited and ministerial. When it becomes absolute, it has already denied that right. It is the function of authority to keep life dependent upon God, and to that end to reverence and cherish those forward and upward movements of life in which the will of God is gradually declared. It is the temptation of authority to despise life or to ignore it, to identify its own momentary will with the ultimate will of God, and so to become itself, and to force those whom it mechanically controls to become, independent of that will of God which ever inspires man's spiritual growth and seeks expression through it.

You have been condemned as the enemy of religious authority, indeed as the enemy of religion itself, because you have sought to recall authority to the sources of its strength and thus to restore to religious unity a world which existing forms and methods of authority have been for long, and are now ever more and more rapidly, reducing to religious disintegration and decay. You will not be arrested in the work of enduring pith and moment to which you have been called, by this fiat of a day. Through you the dawn has at last broken for thousands of wearied souls who have battled all their lives, and battled hopelessly, with the spectres of doubt and darkness. You have spoken for them the word of hope, so simple and obvious that, till you spoke it with the calm confidence of assured conviction, they dared not believe it to be true : " The present is older and wiser and better than the past which it incorporates and transcends." They will be with you in the long and patient effort, which you will not abandon or relax, to save the majestic and glorious tradition of Roman Christianity from the narrow-hearted and ineffectual isolation from the living world to which it would condemn itself.

It is indeed a long and patient effort that the present situation and the present needs of the religious world demand from those who would keep alive the flame of Christian faith. It is easy to rebel. It is not so easy to hold one's ground and to maintain a living and effective protest in the name of the future against the tyrannous inertia of the past. Yet that is the task of the religious reformer of to-day. The easy solution of a violent schism is no longer possible. It seems indeed to the outside world, which, if it cherishes the religious tradition in nothing else, still clings at least to the scholastic distinction of an absolutely true and an absolutely false, as if no course were open to those who reject the prevailing intellectual theories and concepts of their religious communion but open rebellion and schism. That most costing and courageous attitude of patient loyalty in and through conflict still seems to the world quixotic and unintelligible in religious matters, even while the same world understands and admires in secular affairs the finely-tempered patriotism which reveals itself in some momentary opposition to national madness or even in lifelong opposition to a mistaken national policy. None the less it is the only attitude which the modern view of religion renders possible or even imaginable. Religion is the one universal or rather universalising expression of the human soul. In spite of its actual variety, it is coming consciously to seek a tolerant and understanding unity as its greatest need. Nay, we can now even see that through its very variety it has in the past been unconsciously straining towards a worthy and acceptable unity. It is not at such a moment that schism can be accepted as a solution of differences in the intellectual interpretation of faith. For faith which constitutes religion is one, and will be more and more felt to be one. Theology which interprets religion may be one also. But it will be one only in the provisional results which from time to time it may reach, and to reach those results at all it will demand as conditions the variety and freedom which are given in life itself. No power can resist the unity to which religious faith is tending or the variety and freedom through which alone it will assert and secure its unity.

And with the disappearance of schism as a satisfying expedient of religious reform, there disappears also that which once justified schism and even made it necessary, the absolute claim of any passing form or expression of Catholic Truth to be the sole, necessary, and indisputable form or expression—a claim which is itself essentially uncatholic, sectarian, and schismatic. You have taught us both the necessity of an organised religious system and its inevitable imperfection as something whose life and growth forbid finality, petrifaction, and exclusiveness, and demand elasticity and an unlimited power of assimilation. You have shown us how the religious life, like every other expression of life whatsoever, must seek the universal through self-limitation within the particular.

You have reminded us that the religious life always grows up into the religious system and receives from it in turn the inspiration and the assurance of its own enlarging reach. But you have shown us also how the society may harden itself into knotty growths which reject and rebuke the sap of life, how the particular which began by expressing the universal may end by suppressing it. We are at a crisis of growth where many antinomies of the past are struggling to penetrate and transcend one another in a new and original vital effort. In the sphere of religion the mould of the new form, and much too that is most generous in the forces which will fill it, have been preserved for us by the Catholicity of Rome. But assuredly to that new synthesis Protestantism also will contribute something which will prove that its courageous witness of four centuries to the freedom of the spirit has not been in vain.

It is because the Anglicanism in which I have found my own spiritual home has tenaciously held to both of these apparently contradictory principles, liberty and authority, in virtue of an instinct deeper than its intellectual grasp of the method of their reconciliation, that I have dared to hope that the great constructive enterprise which you have taken in hand might find the most immediate and sympathetic recognition within our own borders. We have idly dreamed of a Reunion which would have sacrificed all the hard gains of life and even life itself to the exigencies of an absolutism henceforward unassailable because at last universal. You have opened up for us the path to a Reunion which would preserve everything that life has acquired, and strengthen it against sterility on the one hand and disintegration on the other and against the decay which is the inevitable issue of both.

For these reasons I offer you across the demolished barrier of a merely defensive and controversial theology this tribute of my admiration and regard. If the writer and thinker who has illustrated our English tongue in building up the splendid fabric of a new and universal human hope should find the tribute unworthy, the warm-hearted and tolerant friend will yet consent to receive it.

Your grateful and devoted friend,

A. L. LILLEY.

PREFACE

I AM indebted to the Editors of the *Commonwealth* and the *Guardian* for their kindness in authorising my use of the articles (forming part of this book) which appeared in the pages of those reviews, and to the Editor of the *Nation* for his kind permission to reprint the article on " M. Desjardins and M. Loisy," which appeared in the *Speaker*. The article on " Mr. Inge and M. Loisy " was written immediately after the publication of Dr. Inge's " Faith and Knowledge," but has not hitherto been published. The chapter on " The Church of England and the Church of France " is taken from a lecture delivered to the members of the Guild of St. Matthew. The rest of the book is new.

Except for a very few verbal alterations, the chapters which make up this volume preserve their original form as magazine articles. Both the narrative of facts and the judgments upon them followed in each case close upon the facts themselves ; and the volume aims at preserving this contemporary character, even at the risk of exposing occasional mistakes of judgment both of men and things. Forecasts of the future, whether about facts or persons, are always dangerous ; but both facts and persons have here for the most part manifested such consistency as to reduce that danger to its lowest terms.

The dates in the margin fix the time of original publication of the separate chapters.

A. L. L.

January, 1908.

CONTENTS

PART I.—LITERATURE OF MODERNISM

xvii

PART I

Literature of Modernism

MODERNISM

INTRODUCTORY

DURING the past ten years, and especially during the last five, the movement which the recent Encyclical has condemned under the name of Modernism has been gradually gathering force and volume throughout those sections of the Roman Communion which are most open to the living influences of the time.

Most of the papers which are here collected have appeared during the last five years in various magazines and reviews as occasional notices of its progress. They were written to call the attention of members of my own Communion to a theological movement which seemed to me, both by the freedom of its method and the boldness of its conclusions, to have more promise of religious fruitfulness than any which had found clear and articulate expression within our own borders. I knew indeed how many among ourselves, and especially among our younger men, were feeling their way to an application of the same apologetic method ; and I hoped that an example of courage and faithfulness in the pursuit of truth which had been an inspiration and encouragement to myself might encourage and inspire them also. Relations of personal friendship with some of the men to whose writings I thus called attention, and an intimate knowledge of, and sympathy with, the hopes and aims of all, warranted me in trusting that I had generally interpreted their thought as faithfully as it is given to one mind to interpret the thought of another. It seemed, therefore, that these collected papers might provide a record, however fragmentary and incomplete, of the movement, and that that record might be useful at a critical moment in its fortunes. One other merit I can claim for them as an exposition of the attitude of the writers with whom they deal. They do not contain, I trust, a single note of the astonishment which is often expressed at the stubborn faithfulness to Rome of men who are labouring to restrain the excesses of Roman authority, and who have reaped for all result condemnation at its hands. That faithfulness maintained hitherto, and which will be maintained in spite of excommunication and anathema, is to me the most intelligible and the most necessary expression of their religious attitude. To the Church which would drive them out with execrations as its most formidable enemies, they turn with the words of unhesitating faith, "Ad quem ibimus? Verba vitæ æternæ habes." We, too, if the like circumstances should arise for us, must be able to say the same words to the Church of our baptism. For we adhere each of us to his special communion, not because of its temporary theological or ecclesiastical system, but because it has the words of eternal life, and because it has created in us a habit of the soul by which it can best mediate them to us.

I ought to add that I have not thought it necessary to include, except in one instance, such notices as I had written of English Modernist writings. Those writings

are, indeed, among the most important contributions to
the literature of the movement, but they are happily too
familiar to the English reader to need introduction or
comment of mine.

I

What is, perhaps, further desirable is some connected
account of the inspiration and aims of the movement by
way of introduction to these straggling notices of it. And,
first of all, the inspiration of Modernism is primarily and
pre-eminently religious. Its leaders, born intellectually
into an age of positivism and metaphysical and religious
scepticism, were early oppressed with a sense of the
contemptuous aloofness of the contemporary world from
the Church. They beheld the educated world estranged
from the Church in a mood of defiant scepticism, or
returning to it occasionally in a mood of despairing
scepticism. They missed everywhere the spontaneous
and joyous energy of unhesitating faith. They noted
with mingled dismay and revulsion of feeling the respectable adhesion of worldly and faithless coteries to the
Church as to a powerful social institution or as to an ark
of social safety from the threatening and revolutionary
movements of the time. They felt that the Church was
unconsciously ceasing to be religious, and was coming to
be exploited as a refuge by all the honest or cowardly
reactions of the moment. Meanwhile they saw the great
mass of the common people become more and more
indifferent and even hostile to such religious witness as
the Church still upheld.

Yet they knew and felt, with an invincible personal

certainty, that the Church had the words of eternal life.
And they, members of the Roman Church, of that Church
which held unchallenged for herself and ministered to all
alien Communions the tradition of the saints and mystics
of Christendom, felt that Rome above all could claim the
priceless heritage of those words. But her possession of
them seemed for the moment futile. She formally recited
them in a language which no one could understand. She
had lost the gift of tongues, the power of effective interpretation. And she had lost it because she refused to
learn the language of those to whom her message was
addressed. If the world had abandoned her, it was
because she had first abandoned the world and condemned
it. The world was alive in thought and action, and she
had chosen to dwell among the tombs of the past. She
who ought to have been the first-fruits of every resurrection of history, anathematised the world because it had
escaped from the tomb of a dead mode of thought and
action, and insisted that there alone was rest and safety.
But these, her faithful sons, believed that she too would
rise again, and in preparing that resurrection they were
confident that they were preparing a new hope for the
world.

But further, their Catholic heritage in Rome justified
of itself every instance of their faith in the religious value
of unfettered thought and new knowledge, and of itself
rebuked the official exclusiveness and sectarianism of a
moment, even if that moment had been four centuries
long. They claimed, and not without reason, that
Catholicism meant before everything else the recognition
and vital reconciliation of the absolute and contingent

elements in human experience. Their chief indictment against Protestantism was that it had confused the boundaries between these two elements. Catholicism, with its implicit, if not always explicit, faith in a growing Divine revelation, could afford to distinguish, even if at times it had failed to do so, between the absolute spirit of that revelation and the contingent forms in which it had from time to time expressed itself. Protestantism, in its anxiety to preserve some fixed and authoritative nucleus of belief, had chosen arbitrarily among its contingent forms and given to some of them an absolute value. In the Protestant the scholar and the believer were often at odds, with the result that the scholar was sometimes forced to compromise his most certain conclusions so as to harmonise them with the claims of the believer. In the Catholic the scholar and the believer could live together in peace, since the scholar knew that he was merely establishing the phenomenal events or contingent forms in which the believer had found, or through which he had expressed, the realities of faith. The Protestant was always timidly attempting to guarantee the absolute of faith by some historical or philosophical contingency. The Catholic had been trained to find the absolute of faith in that to which the universal conscience of humanity witnessed, " *quod semper, quod ubique, quod ab omnibus.*" And if the growth and deepening of knowledge had impressed upon him the certainty that that absolute had never been and could never be perfectly and exhaustively mediated through the contingent fact and thought of a world in growth, he was not in the slightest degree disconcerted.

For in the Church, the organ and instrument of the Eternal Christ, the absolute was for ever descending into and incarnating itself in the relative ; the relative was continually ascending into and incorporating itself with the absolute.   In a word, the object of religious faith retains its absolute character in the life of will and conscience, of aspiration and prayer.   The moment it comes out into the open and begins to be mediated through thought, it takes on perforce something of a relative character. Catholicism, in its widest and fullest sense, is but the growing realization and effectuation of the principle of religious growth.   Founded in the absolute of faith given in varying degrees in human life as the necessary condition of that life, its heart is open to recognize and welcome, its mind to co-ordinate and utilize, all the spiritual treasure of humanity.   For it Christianity is the resuming and controlling moment of a process of self-revelation of the Divine which has been continuous with the spiritual growth of humanity.   It is at once an act of incorporation of the revelation of the past, and a point of departure for the revelation of the future.

With this conception of what Catholicism is, and an intense belief in the mission and the capacity of Rome to give effect to it, the Modernist Catholics have not so much framed a new kind of apologetic as conceived in a new way the very nature of apologetic.   The apologetic of the past has too often repelled the outside world by an appearance of insincerity and chicane.   This appearance was due to the fact that that apologetic had pledged itself to an impossible task.   Identifying the Christian revelation with its expression through a temporary phase of thought and a particular systematization of knowledge, it attempted, in vain, to attach revelation so conceived to a fresh body of knowledge which, under the impulse of new ways of thinking, was systematizing itself on different lines.   The clumsiness of the sutures was too obvious, and besides they gave way after a very little wear.   But the Modernist conception of revelation has given a new character and method to apologetic.   If revelation is given in life and through life, if all life is in various degrees and on various levels the obedient or recalcitrant medium of revelation, if the natural is dependent upon and penetrated by the supernatural, then apologetic ceases to be mere intellectual fence and defence, and becomes instead living interpretation.   The first duty of the apologist is to understand his own time, its profoundest aspirations, its most enduring hopes, its most generous and unselfish activities, its most disinterested quest of truth.   It is through union with these forms and qualities of life that even the classical revelation of the past gains new fruitfulness and power.   And so apologetic, to be efficient, must be vital and not merely formal.   It must interpret the revelation in terms of the concrete life of the present, and not be content to juggle with contemporary knowledge till it yields a deceptive show of agreement with some past form of revelation which has been given an absolute value.

And here it may be well to take account of that indictment which has been so abundantly laid against the Modernist theology, that it has pronounced an unnatural divorce between faith and knowledge.   Modernism claims, it is said, to preserve intact all the affirmations of faith, while lightly admitting certain results of knowledge which ought to be destructive of those affirmations. Now this, it seems to me, is an almost wanton misrepresentation of the distinction between faith and knowledge which the Modernists have attempted to draw. For that distinction is purely one of fact. It depends, no doubt, to some degree, upon a particular philosophic conception of the position and function of the understanding in the total economy of the human spirit. That philosophic bias they could not, as men of their time, altogether escape. But independently of it the distinction asserts itself as one of fact. The affirmations of faith are, as a matter of fact, independent of, and vitally prior to, the rational process. They are indeed not irrational : so far from that they are, and just because they are affirmations of the total human spirit, charged with an implicit reason. Those affirmations find their occasion in certain facts and aspects of the phenomenal world, and it is the business of the rational intelligence to develop their rational content in closest vital touch with the facts and aspects of fact which provoked them. And as increasing knowledge means a more accurate perception of fact and a juster view of the general relations of fact, it is certain that it must not only affect the form of faith, but even assist in evoking its rational content.

It is exactly this close interdependence of faith and knowledge that every Modernist writer most positively asserts. It is the chief burden of his offence in the eyes of scholastic orthodoxy. For it there can be no vital interdependence between them, for the simple reason that for it they are identical, faith being given as complete and imperfectible knowledge. Yet the Modernist holds that a distinction remains in the fact that faith has a vital priority to all reasoned knowledge. In all its affirmations there remains an element which is un-analysable by reason, or at least which has not yet been analysed by it. And if the reason could complete that analysis, it would die of its own too much. We should know as God knows, and there being no task left for the reason to accomplish, it would perish of its very success.

But it is not merely from intellectual considerations that the Modernist infers the distinction between faith and knowledge. He finds it given in the evidence of religion itself as to the nature of its own certainties. The religious knowledge of God, for instance, is not the comprehension or acceptance of some intellectual proof of the necessity of His existence, but the immediate personal sense of Him as Inspirer, Redeemer, Judge. The really saving knowledge of God is possessed, and in abundant measure, by many a soul which is incapable of appraising the force of such intellectual proofs, even by many a soul which has never heard of them. Or again, those proofs may have a compelling validity for the mind without conveying any knowledge of God which can stir the soul into life. Or yet again, they may altogether fail to satisfy the mind, while in spite of their failure, and of the failure of all other formal proofs, the soul is pro-foundly conscious of God as the very source and substance of its life. Religion rightly takes no account of any faith which has not this elemental certainty. It even asks for no other save when it is mounted on the stilts of a dog-matic orthodoxy. If the Modernist distinguishes between faith and knowledge, he does so not to deny the legitimate action of reason in the service of faith, but to protest against their illegitimate confusion by the scholastic. And again, wherein he distinguishes between them, he points for his justification to the evidence of vital religion itself.

But while the Modernist insists upon the priority of religion as spiritual fact to all intellectual translations of it, upon its development through spiritual action and not through passive submission to an intellectual necessity, upon its origin in spirit and its growth in spirit, he does not deny either the necessity or the value of an external religious authority in forming the life of the soul. But here again he finds that authority in the vital influences of spirit rather than in formal conceptions as to its nature and method of action. For the Modernist the Church is primarily a home of the spirit. It is the spiritual atmosphere which as Christians we breathe ; it is a highway across the desert of life built up out of all the heroisms, sacrifices, martyrdoms of the Christian centuries whereon all the pilgrims of faith may march with confidence ; it is the spiritual soil in which we are rooted, and in which, as we grow spiritually, our roots strike more widely and deeply. Its organ of authority exists, or ought to exist, in order to recover and concentrate at a fixed point of self-consciousness the spiritual power diffused throughout the whole mass, and to mediate it again by a thousand living processes to each unit of the mass. That diffused power, which it is the function of authority to mediate to each Christian soul, is the generalized tradition of Christian life, the certainties

which have grown out of and been enriched by the
religious experience of the Christian Society—tradition
and certainties which have their vital source and their
eternal norm in the Gospel, in the life and Person of Jesus
Christ.   And here again the Modernist is at issue with
the Intellectualist.   For the latter holds that the Gospel
was once reduced to an adequate intellectual form, and
that that form was entrusted to the safekeeping of certain
official guardians whose function it is to impose it upon
the faithful, who are faithful only when they accept it
without questioning.   The Intellectualist, indeed, need
not always be so logical, but he has for once reached the
end of his logical tether in the conception and spirit of
actual Roman authority.   The Modernist, on the other
hand, believes that because the Gospel was life, and more
abundant life, it was bound to commit itself freely to all
the risks of life.   He conceives of the Church as the Gospel
taking those vital risks, as the Gospel actually lived by
saintly souls, and of its authority as the mediation of
that abundant life to its already living and therefore
receptive members.

II

It has been necessary, in order to do justice to the
Modernists, to insist at some length on their interior view
of religion which places them in the direct line of spiritual
succession from the Mystics.   But they have one
characteristic which distinguishes them from the less
intelligible and more repellent aspects of Mysticism, and
which ought of itself to have protected them against
the charge of instituting a divorce between faith and

knowledge. They have an almost passionate faith in the value to religion of actual contemporary knowledge, and of the devotion to the living quest of truth by which it is obtained. Not only is there nothing about them of that contempt for modern knowledge and ways of thinking so laboriously flaunted by the devout votaries of Roman scholasticism, and even feebly imitated by scholastics who are not Roman, but they are conspicuous among theologians of all Christian communions for their eager and enthusiastic confidence in the achievements of the modern mind. They value, indeed, the thought of the past, but they value it as the seed out of which the thought of the present has grown, or as the food on which the thinker of the present has been nourished so that his thought in turn may be vigorous and individual. In short they do not conceive of thought as stored-up treasure, but as fructifying seed and fruitful harvest, as nourishing food and the intellectual health and robustness which it produces. No intellectual acquisition of the past has any value save in so far as it points the way to further acquisition. Nor can the excellence of the past seed be allowed to weigh against the insignificance of the present growth. In this matter a live dog is better than a dead lion. After all, health depends even more upon the reality of the living process than upon what comes of it.

So, conceiving of thought and knowledge in this vital way, the Modernists are frankly and without reserve the intellectual children of their time. They have, as we have seen, turned almost every suggestion of modern specula-tion to account in their analysis of the content of faith,

and in their working theory of its relations to knowledge.
They have seen the necessity of accepting certain general
conclusions of criticism as to the origin and historical
character and value of the books of Holy Scripture. Some
of them, indeed, have been among the most fearless
pioneers in that field. They are satisfied that theology
must for the future make its account with the composite
view of the Hexateuch and of the prophetic writings
which criticism has established. They accept the view
of the theological purpose and symbolical method of the
author of the fourth Gospel, and see in his work rather a
construction of faith than a record of fact. They find
even in the Synoptics distinct traces of the theological
and ecclesiastical preoccupations of the second Christian
generation, and turn to St. Mark and to the passages
which St. Matthew and St. Luke have in common for the
original nucleus of the Gospel record.

Again, in the field of Church history they fearlessly
apply critical methods of historical investigation. As a
result they have undermined the merely statical view of
Church organization, and revealed the ecclesiastical
system as a natural growth determined by the supernatural needs and occasions of the Church's life. They
have transformed hagiology, and removed by skilful
critical surgery that overgrowth of legend which had
defaced the body of Christian history and become one of
the greatest offences to the religious sense of our time.
And, most important gain of all, they have established
as an objective fact of history the growth of dogma, its
growth within the limits of the Biblical record, and its
growth in the historical life of the Church. It is a

revolution which they have accomplished in the view of the historical character and fortunes of the Church. Yet it is a revolution which they believe to be entirely salutary to religion. Their faith in the Divine action includes and necessitates a desire to know as accurately as the best available methods of enquiry will enable them to know, the actual facts through which that action was manifested. Their desire to reach objective certainty is as conspicuously sincere as their use of the methods by which our generation strives to attain it is conspicuously honest. For both the sincerity of the one and the honesty of the other are expressions of their religious faith. They believe that God is the Truth of Spirit which acts through facts and through our reasoned attempts to establish the vital order of fact, and therefore they believe in the spiritual service of both truth of fact and truth of reason. Truth of fact must always be accordant with truth of spirit; and it is the honest attempt to know the truth of fact, and to discover through such knowledge the law or method of action of that truth of spirit which was already immediately revealed in fact, that constitutes the truth of reason. It is the truth of spirit that is given immediately in faith. It is the truth of fact that critical history attempts to establish. The perfect truth of reason would be the absolute knowledge of how spirit works throughout the whole order of fact, or of how every detail of fact strikes some necessary note in the total harmony of spirit. And as we cannot attain to such absolute knowledge, the truth of reason is for us just such hints and instances of the law of spirit as we can surprise. It is from this point of view that the

Modernists seek not only without fear, but with unhesitating confidence, to utilize the best contemporary knowledge in the service of religion.

But once more they have welcomed the results of the modern comparative study of religions, not grudgingly as of embarrassing knowledge, but gratefully as of knowledge which serves to illustrate and confirm the assertions of faith. They see in those alien religions other revelations of God, the Divine Spirit sustaining and nourishing like dispositions and receptivities to our own into diverse realizations of the same hidden ground of reality in life. But they see in them also the same revelation, the same power of God working through so many different types of racial character, phases and degrees of knowledge, and practical habit, the Eternal Word dispensing His Light wherever light is found. They reflect how much religion has already gained from such knowledge when they recall the theory of diabolic imitation which seemed necessary to the pious and charitable souls who first came into contact with the religions of the East to account for facts so unexpected and disconcerting.

The Modernist movement has introduced a new note into the Roman Communion. Among vast numbers of the clergy of France and Italy especially, the life of the study has become the natural pendant to the life of prayer. In no other communion of the Christian world is there such a ferment of thought about the things of religion, or such an earnest and serious pursuit of positive knowledge. Even Protestant Germany, which has so honestly laboured in the interests of theological progress for a whole century, is turning with astonishment and

admiration to this veritable renaissance in Rome. It
remembers that it at least enjoyed the freedom of the
University chair in attempting the work of theological
renewal. But here are men who have to work under the
jealous and uninterrupted surveillance of reactionary
Orders, or in some petty seminary professorship, or amid
conditions of solitude and poverty which would rebuke
all but the bravest and most enthusiastic spirits. And
yet they have never compromised their vision of truth
nor minimised the conclusions which the ascertained facts
forced upon them. They are sustained by a simple and
passionate love of truth, and by the certainty which fills
them with a kind of despotic inspiration that all truth is
of God. For them the results of positive theology seem
to blend almost naturally and without effort with the
immediate certainties of mystical religion. They possess
that peculiar chemistry of the spirit which men seem to
acquire in crises of enthusiastic faith, and which har-
monises the most conflicting elements of their knowledge
in a generous and satisfying unity. It is on this account
that they not only have succeeded in discovering the
religious value of the new learning for themselves, but
are undoubtedly destined to be its spiritual sponsors
with every communion in Christendom.

Nor must it be forgotten that the Modernist Catholic
has a special encouragement and inspiration in his
devotion to knowledge. He can remind himself that he
has had innumerable precursors in every special phase of
his own thought and knowledge throughout the whole
past of Catholicism. In the sphere of apologetic, his
thought was suggested long ago by Duns Scotus and

Pascal, and is even implicit in the whole mystic conception of religion which has nowhere been so richly exemplified as in Rome. He does not forget that the science of Biblical criticism had its birth in his own Communion, through the labours of Simon and Astruc. When he turns to the history of dogma, he fortifies himself not only with the recent memory of Newman, but with the suggestive fore-gleams of Petavius and Thomassin. In his attempt to write ecclesiastical history honestly, he works under the high patronage of a long Benedictine and Bollandist tradi-tion. And when he recognizes the revelational value of non-Christian religions, he can go back to the very begin-nings of Christianity for the most unhesitating sanction of his intelligence and charity in Justin Martyr and Clement of Alexandria. The assertions of faith are so broad and deep that they thus sometimes seem unconsciously to predict occasions and forms of knowledge which have not yet appeared. And indeed, it is not mere seeming, for does not faith always say something more and greater than it knows ?

III

But there is one aspect of Modernism, perhaps the most important, which seems to have escaped those among ourselves who have professed an interest in its fortunes. What, they ask, is the attitude of the Modernist with regard to this doctrine or to that ? Does he really believe in the Divinity of our Lord, or in miracles, or in some other affirmation of dogma arbitrarily selected as a test of orthodoxy ? The habit of mind out of which such questions can arise is too obviously obtuse to the whole

Modernist position. It takes for granted that Christian dogma is a mathematical sum of truths, some of which are so unimportant that they may be discarded without injury to the whole, while others have been finally given in an essential and intangible form. Now Modernism is above all things the denial that dogma is a sum of truths. It insists that dogma is a body of truth, fashioned by the soul of truth which inhabits it, and in turn providing that soul with a means of expression. And so it is not concerned to discard any dogma as valueless, or to select any as specially indispensable. It is concerned only to connect all alike with the life of faith, with that immediate sense of the Divine action and revelation in life which is the very heart of religion.

It is impossible for anyone who does not realize that Modernism is the attempt to reach a new theological synthesis to be at all just to its claims and achievements. That attempt has been forced upon the Christian theologian by the revolution in our world-view which has been wrought in quite recent times by the accumulated effect of a revolutionary physical science, a revolutionary method of establishing historical truth, and a revolutionary psychology. Two other great syntheses have preceded it—the synthesis in terms of a Platonic or neo-Platonic world-view which was completed by the sixth Christian century, and the synthesis in terms of a world-view mediated through Aristotelian intellectualism which was perfected by St. Thomas before the end of the thirteenth century. The intervals between these critical moments in theological development have been occupied by local and particular skirmishes in various parts of the theological field. They have been the periods of partial heresies. But the great crises themselves have been moments of general reconstruction for which the particular speculation had prepared. How difficult it has been for official authority to recognize the near approach of these critical moments and their constructive significance may be gathered from a Letter* of Gregory IX, which has been quoted in the recent Encyclical of Pius X in support of the latter's condemnation of Modernism. Yet—who would believe it ? —the Modernism which Gregory IX condemned in 1228 was that very Aristotelian apologetic which long before the century's end was to receive its classical form through the intellectual labours of St. Thomas, and whose canonical value Pius X is now once again attempting to impose upon Christendom. Within a few years Gregory IX had to retract his condemnation of the Aristotelian philosophy, and to approve its use in the schools of the Church. The Modernism of to-day may have to wait longer for its vindication, but that vindication will come. The mind of the thirteenth century, dominated by the need of applying its logical categories to the whole sum of its knowledge, could remain no longer satisfied with a Christianity whose truths maintained an arbitrary aloofness from the rest of knowledge. So the twentieth century will be unable to apprehend Christian truth at all save through those categories of growth and development which it is learning to apply to all the objects of its knowledge. It is from the logical

* *Epistola ad magistros theologiæ Parisienses.* The document is given in Denzinger's " Enchiridion," 5th edition, p. 139. Denzinger dates the Epistle 1223 by mistake.

and mathematical categories of Aristotelianism that we
inherit the notion of a sum of particular Christian truths
with various degrees of deductive validity.   Modernism
can only conceive of particular truths as they are part of
the truth, and of their validity as the degree of their vital
participation in and illustration of *the* truth.   And that
truth is the vision of the Divine action vouchsafed to a
religious sense inherent in man, which we call faith, and
mediated to us through a world of fact which exists as a
growing order, and through the Divine-human life in
which the spiritual secret of that order was supremely
revealed.   There is no dogma, therefore, which can resist
the solvent of analysis necessitated by the application to
it of the category of growth.   But neither is there any
which does not in some way witness to truth, and to some
degree inhere in truth, by reason of the fact that it has
had its origin in some profound experience of the general
soul of man which is the divinely-constituted source of
all revelation.   So Modernism rejects no dogma and
transforms all.

As yet, however, this new synthesis makes no claim to
completeness.   It is, indeed, not so much a synthesis at
all as the obedience to a despotic impulse towards one.
One thing only can be prophesied of it, but that may be
prophesied with certainty.   The track which it is clearing
for theology is the only one which theology can safely
follow in the coming days.   And in clearing that track,
it is preparing a mutual intelligence between the sundered
branches of Christendom which is possible on no other
terms.   Protestant theology, which was scholastic to the
core, separated from the main body of the Christian

tradition in refusing adhesion to certain dogmas as intellectually false, as out of accord with the revelation given in Scripture intellectually conceived and interpreted. Protestantism, indeed, as a religious movement, had gone deeper than its apologetics admitted. It had really denied certain dogmas because religious experience seemed to prove them valueless and even injurious to the life of religion. But Modernism holds that life may be trusted to slough its old skin, and that when it does so in obedience to the needs of nature it may find that every expression of the old life needs to repeat itself in some worthier and more developed form in the new. With the sense of the absoluteness of God's self-revelation in life, of the supremacy of the life and Spirit of Jesus Christ as the norm of that revelation, and of the relative value of all its various forms as it expresses itself through the religious life and thought of humanity, all motives to schism will have vanished. In proportion as these conceptions gain ground, and they cannot by their very nature gain ground in one Christian communion without affecting all, the reunion of Christendom will pass from the stage of a vague sentimental desire to that of a rational and highly practical aim.

CHAPTER I

M. DENIS ON CHURCH AND STATE IN FRANCE

October 29,
1902

HISTORY, which is full of ironies, has seldom surely known a greater or a more tragic than the present position of affairs in France. Of almost forty millions of Frenchmen not quite a million are Protestant, and, probably, not more than three millions are definitely non-Catholic. The monarchic absolutism of the seventeenth century procured for France, by however questionable means, a political and religious unity elsewhere unknown. The political unity still survives in the centralized administration which persists through every change in the form of government. The political heredity of France declares itself in an ingrained suspicion of variety, in a temperament which makes the liberty she cherishes as an ideal impossible as a fact. And, equally, religious unity is a first principle of her national consciousness. It shows how deeply the inheritance of the *Grand Siècle* has passed into her being, that she cannot even now regard the religious descendants of Calvin—whom M. Brunetière himself has described as a typical exponent of the French genius in matters of theology—as other than foreigners in the land of their birth and origin. Yet it is in this supremely Catholic country that a savage anti-clericalism rages; that the gasconade of the atheist lecture-hall or the Masonic lodge has become a settled principle of government; that the Church is preparing to fight in

24

her last ditch the battle of religious education ; that the Government which had just passed a most stringent law intended to clip the wings of the great religious orders, if not altogether to crush out their life, was yet able to secure a sweeping majority at the polls ; that a *quondam* seminarist has been deliberately chosen to accomplish the work of destruction which it seems doubtful whether even his clumsy haste will be able to arrest or delay.

A situation so ironical compels reflection, and clamours for explanation. It will not do to accept in explanation the tradition of militant English Protestantism that the French Church is corrupt. Besides that it is exceedingly vague—as, indeed, it is probably meant to be—such a charge is from every point of view so lacking in support that it can only be described as ludicrously and scandalously false. Perhaps in no part of Christendom is a body of men to be found of simpler and more self-denying lives, more wholly devoted to their duties, more conscious of the spiritual character of their mission, and, at the same time, more intelligent of the simple human aspect of its claims and more capable in discharging them, than the French clergy. One has only to consult the evidence of capable, conscientious, and unprejudiced Englishmen like Mr. Hamerton and Mr. Bodley, who know (or have known) France intimately, or, better still, to recall the *bons prêtres* of French fiction from Balzac down to M. Bourget, M. Ferdinand Fabre, M. Lafargue, and M. Fonsegrive, to see how ignorant and absurd are these charges of corruption. Nor will it be sufficient, though it may be more true, to say that the French laity are largely divorced from the Church. Such a charge is

probably no more true and no less true of France than
of any other country in Europe—of Germany, say, or of
England. Membership in the Church has at all times,
and in all countries, had a twofold aspect. For an elect
few it has meant the development of the life of the
spirit. For the great majority it has meant the hope of
avoiding the dreaded consequences of the life of the
flesh. Probably France still produces as many saints
as ever she did. Equally probably, as few of her children
as ever are ready to face the terrors of the future without
recourse to the Church's supernatural assistance.

Yet this much-talked-of divorce of the laity from the
Church—too true, alas! even of England, America, and
Germany—is in one important respect still more true
of France. And it is that aspect of the divorce which
is the real explanation of the present relations of French
civil government and French religion. While Frenchmen still, for the most part, seek to insure themselves
through the instrumentality of the Church against the
risks of the future, they just as generally regard all the
interests of the present life as being entirely outside the
Church's ken. They resent the influence of the clergy
in temporal affairs as an unwarranted incursion of
foreigners within their own frontiers. Rightly or wrongly,
they believe that the clergy do not understand, and
have no desire to understand, the lay point of view.
And so they have come instinctively to suspect every
attempted exercise of clerical influence as being necessarily inspired either by ignorance or by craft. Now,
it might not be difficult to estimate the share of the laity
in the responsibility for this estrangement. But,

assuredly, the responsibility is not entirely with them. And in the remarkable pamphlet of the Abbé Denis, published in the early months of this year, we have the indictment of the Church for her contribution to so disastrous a result, drawn up by one of her most faithful and devoted sons. That it has been drawn up with such insight, such sincerity, and such courage by one of the most prominent of the younger clergy in France is, perhaps, the best guarantee that the estrangement of the clergy and the laity on all the great questions of living moment, political, social, and intellectual, is by no means inevitable, and even that it may be already beginning to disappear.

M. Denis is the director of the *Annales de Philosophie Chrétienne*, a review which, under his direction, has become almost the official organ of theological Liberalism in the Church of France. To the English reader of M. Bourget's novels, it may convey more to say that M. Denis is the Abbé Chanut of " L'Étape," the latest surprise which the author of " Le Disciple " has given us. But M. Denis is very far indeed from being the mere dupe of generous illusions, which M. Bourget, in the mood of pessimism with which his so recent religious orthodoxy seems to have inspired him, portrays in the Abbé Chanut. No one could be more free from the fatal illusions in which M. Bourget seems anxious to encourage the Church than is M. Denis. No one could have demonstrated with more clearness and more courage than he how fatal these illusions have been, how still more fatal they may become if persisted in. It needs the courage of absolute sincerity to speak home truths like these :—

" Catholicism in Latin countries has reached a lamentable pass. It must adapt itself to its environment, or it will continue to decay. That is the least pessimistic forecast. With us the Church is not suffering from schism, but from inanition. What we want is not so much unity as vitality. We are disobedient, not to our masters in the supernatural order, but to liberty in the natural order. We are languishing because we have refused the discipline of action, and accepted a lifeless immobility within the discipline of dogma. Dogma is a light to lead us on. We have made it a barrier beyond which we must not go. We have become helots in the twentieth century because of our desire that the past should live again. We have no relations with anything that is vital, neither with science, nor with society, nor with the State. We are crushed by our political traditionalism, which we make an article of faith. We are compromised by our formalism, which is becoming more and more unintelligible, because we substitute it too often for the spirit which makes alive, even for the Gospel itself. We love the Church and its infallible *magisterium*, but on condition that the Church dispenses us from the need of acting, of thinking, of knowing, of loving what is undoubtedly good in our time. The evil is in us. Let us not look for it elsewhere. Let us not be like those invalids who rebel against the advice of the doctor, and throw out of the window the remedies which would restore them, but to which in their folly they attribute their suffering. The evil is in ourselves, and has sunk deep to the innermost recesses of our being."

There is the weakness of the Church. She has withdrawn

from the common life. The indictment is summed up in a phrase. The clergy are "*hommes de sacristie*"— *voilà tout*. They have failed to understand the needs of the society to which they have had to minister. They have thought that it was sufficient to impose the faith upon an indifferent world. They have made no attempt to appreciate the causes of its indifference, or to prepare the way for its intelligent acceptance of the faith. For a hundred years France has been living under a Parliamentary Government. For a hundred years the Church has sought to identify the Faith with suspicion and defiance of Parliamentarism, and for thirty years with hatred of Republicanism and hopeless championship of some form of absolutism. Devoted sons of tradition and of doctrinal authority, the clergy have not learned to conform to the methods of Parliamentary compromise which the modern State requires. They have not even bowed to the supreme direction of the Holy See. When two of their number, the Abbé Lemire and the Abbé Gayraud, sought and obtained seats in the Chamber of Deputies as Parliamentary *ralliés* to the Republic, one was deprived of his *celebret*, and the other became the victim of a petty persecution, and found himself forced at the last elections to meet the opposition of a clerical candidate who was politically orthodox. The results of this determination of the Church to sulk in her monarchical tent have been disastrous to her own interests. She has seen interests the most sacred—the family, education, the right of association—revolutionized without any power of interference on her part.

Again, she has refused to understand the power and

the needs of the people. The advent of the great mass of workers to political power, which has constituted what is known as the social question, has been completely disregarded by her. And yet it was supremely her business to understand and to meet this momentous issue.

" Religion," says the Abbé Six, " is summed up in two words, justice and charity. Precisely the two things demanded by the people are justice and charity. . . . Charity has been given by the religious congregations, both men and women, and by all the clergy with an incomparable zeal and devotion. But, besides the people which suffers, which is ill, or has its orphans to be ministered to, there is the people which has strong arms, and works with them. It asks for justice. Now, have we publicly, and as a body, fought and suffered sufficiently to procure justice for the people as our admirable Sisters have toiled and suffered to give it charity ? Have we, as a body, the reputation of being favourable to the just claims of the people ? In a word, are we popular by our defence of justice as the Sisters are by their exercise of charity ? There is the whole question ; and who would dare to answer—Yes ? "

And, again, the clergy have lost their influence by their lack of interest in the intellectual problems which disturb the age. Hear this frank confession of the Abbé Denis, and recognize the community of experience of the teaching Church in presence of the educated laity of all the European nations :—

" The majority of the secular and regular priests are convinced that the problems of evil, of heredity, of

Divine justice, of evolution, of the historical origin of religions, of the sources of Scripture, are completely unknown to their flocks, and that to speak of them is to talk Greek. Fatal ignorance which fosters intellectual apathy among the clergy ! "

But M. Denis at least has no illusions. He knows how intellectually curious the younger generation is. He recognizes the high level of popular education. He knows how various and acute are the intellectual interests of the educated section of modern society, the doctors, officers, advocates, elementary teachers, pupils (male and female) of the lycées and the normal schools. And it is with something like dismay that he contrasts with this high level of knowledge and of intellectual interest the ignorance and intellectual barrenness of the clergy. The priest never thinks of grappling in the pulpit with great intellectual issues. It is not wonderful, perhaps. For there he has before him only pious listeners who know nothing of intellectual struggles. But even if the intelligent were there he would not know how to meet their needs. His seminarist education has not fitted him to get beyond the familiar truths of the catechism and the liturgy. If, in his seminary days, he has ever heard the actual questions of philosophy and science touched upon at all, it was only that they might be dismissed with a sniff of contempt, or crushed with a summary condemnation. No wonder that he is disarmed in presence of objections which he does not understand. It is, perhaps, intelligible that, in presence of this fatal incapacity of the Church to find an entrance for its message into alert and eager minds, it should be with a feeling of something like despair that a faithful son of the Church in France recalls the treatment of her most gifted scholars in the present generation—the Abbé Duchesne suspended from his chair at the Catholic Institute for his critical treatment of history, the Abbé Loisy subjected to censure for his pioneer work in biblical exegesis, and the Abbé Turmel for his study of the origins of dogma. And equally it is with a sense of shame that such a one remembers that the great masters of philosophical apologetics in France during the last ten years have been laymen—M. Fonsegrive, M. Blondel, M. Ollé-Laprune, M. Brunetière, and M. Goyau.

That is the indictment drawn up by M. Denis with a courage in which there is no trace of presumption, with a sincerity which could only be inspired by the most absolute faith in the divine mission of the Church. That there are eyes to see the truth and voices to speak it is surely a most hopeful sign of the future of the Church of France. Still more hopeful is it that the eyes and the voices are so many. The "École Large"—how these names repeat themselves in the history of Christian thought—is already a strong and active advance-guard in the army of the Church of France. In the sphere of Parliamentary action there are still but the Abbé Lemire, the Deputy for Hazebrouck in the Nord, and the Abbé Gayraud, the Deputy for Brest ; but they are a host in themselves. The "Abbés Démocrates," who champion the social movement in the Church with the exuberant vigour and enthusiasm of youth, are making their influence felt on an ever-increasing scale. There is the

Abbé Naudet, with his " Justice Sociale," the Abbés
Klein, Dabry, Six, Sifflet, Garnier, Ardant, and many
more. There is the enthusiastic movement of the
younger laity directed by M. Marc Sangnier and his
colleagues of the " Sillon." The influence of this growing
movement has been solemnly stamped with the seal of
authority by the great Congress, held last January at
Bourges under the presidency of its Archbishop, Mgr.
Servonnet. And, again, the whole question of seminarist
education is passing through a phase of practical reform.
Mgr. Le Camus, the Bishop of La Rochelle, has completely remodelled the teaching of his diocesan seminary.
Mgr. Fuzet, the Archbishop of Rouen, has insisted on
the same need. Above all, the Archbishop of Albi,
Mgr. Mignot, by his discourse on the " Method of
Theology " at the Catholic Institute of Toulouse, has
prepared the way for a really liberal treatment of apologetics in the chairs of Catholic Institutes and Seminaries.
To Albi, it may be said in passing, we owe the philosophic
mind of M. Birot, and to Toulouse the sane and critical
scholarship of M. Batiffol. But, perhaps, there is no
greater or more trustworthy evidence of the strength and
extensive influence of the new movement than the
dismay it has occasioned among the ranks of the old
guard. Mgr. Turinaz, a prelate of strong convictions
and vigorous temper, who has for almost thirty years
ruled the diocese of Nancy, has made himself the official
mouthpiece of the hostility with which the new movement is being met. That hostility had, indeed, already
been uttered with sufficient virulence by Père Fontaine
in his " Infiltrations Protestantes et le Clergé Français."

But those who wish to obtain a rapid and comprehensive view of the nature and variety of this most hopeful movement in the Church of France will find in the vigorous indictment and condemnation of it by Mgr. Turinaz a means ready to their hand.

CHAPTER II

ON the last day of September, in the year 1901, there *November 5,* died in Paris a man who for more than thirty years was, *1902* perhaps, the greatest single influence in moulding the *élite* of the French clergy. He was an Irishman, born at Bodyke so far back as 1829. In 1844 he became a seminarist at Bordeaux, and five years later went to Paris to complete his studies at Saint-Sulpice. There he had hardly been ordained priest when he was appointed to the chair of theology in 1852. For thirty-two years he continued to occupy it, giving himself with an unexampled zeal and a unique power of direction to the great work of that home of theological learning and clerical training. In 1884 he was sent to Boston, in Massachusetts, to found a seminary of the Sulpicians. Five years later he was called to Washington to organize the seminary teaching in connection with the new Roman Catholic University, and once more was he recalled to Boston, in 1894, as Superior of its diocesan seminary.

What were the character and the force of Father Hogan's influence at Saint-Sulpice may be gathered from an excellent appreciation in the *Revue du Clergé Français* for the first *quinzaine* of August, by one of his most distinguished pupils, Mgr. Batiffol, the present rector of the Catholic Institute of Toulouse. Much that is most intimate and characteristic in the influence of a great

teacher can never, alas ! reach beyond the narrow circle
of those who have felt it. But, fortunately, Father
Hogan has left us a precious legacy in his volume, entitled
" Clerical Studies," the matured and mellow fruitage of a
long life of strenuous intellectual energy in uninterrupted
contact with a single practical mission. For here there
is something more than the formal results of a life of
scholarship. There is something of the most intimate
quality of a soul, its freshness, its simplicity, its absolute
sincerity, its obvious sympathy with every natural and
healthy manifestation of life.

But the present interest of this book lies in the evidence
it affords, alike in its own teachings and in the circumstances of its author's position and influence, of the nature
and extent of the recent revival of Catholic theology
in France. That revival, which seems to the foreign
observer to have come with such astonishing suddenness,
was after all being prepared in the silent but far-reaching
influence of teachers like Father Hogan. Only the love
of truth, the keen intellectual sympathy with all the
best knowledge of our time, the sincere and strenuous
endeavour to adapt the content of the Christian revelation
to that knowledge, to which this book bears witness,
could have produced the change of theological method
which has found most adequate expression in the now
famous address of Mgr. Mignot before the Catholic
Institute of Toulouse. What that revival means, how
revolutionary its character, may, perhaps, best be
appreciated by a brief review of the Archbishop of Albi's
thesis. The Archbishop prefaces his quest of an efficient
theological method, of a method which will bring theology

into living correspondence with actual knowledge, by
contrasting the present position of theology with regard
to other sciences with that which obtained in the middle
ages.   During the long development of Christian civiliza-
tion the Western mind has passed through two distinct
phases or stages of evolution, the one deductive and
synthetic, the other experimental and analytic.   The
thirteenth century saw the consummation of the first
stage.   Our own age has witnessed the virtual triumph
of the other.

" Human knowledge was at first a formless and chaotic
mass in which every element was confusedly mingled.
Aristotle's first attempts at organization—themselves far
from complete—had been lost in the vast revolution
which renewed the world after the fall of Rome.   Cut off
from its origins, deprived of every means of information
unskilled as yet in direct observation, and yet unable to
remain inactive, reason had to content itself with hasty
generalizations, embracing as best it might the meagre
baggage of facts and memories which it possessed.   To
this thought, so unsteady, without knowledge of what it
might rest upon for support, Christianity offered the
objective element it needed.   On the one hand the Bible,
on the other dogma tinged with Hellenism through the
medium of the Fathers, provided a chronology and metaphysic which were accepted with confidence, and served
as a framework for further developments.   From this
source it was necessary by force of mere logic to extract
a solution for every problem.   Science was therefore
deductive, and it might be said of it, as of a famous
prisoner, that it was nourished with the blood from its

own veins. Meanwhile, as fresh data arose from the hidden depths of history or of nature, they were made to fit in with the original system. Thus the philosophy of Averroës was assimilated as well as the discoveries of Albertus Magnus. In spite of a method so imperfect, this science of the *Trivium* and *Quadrivium* was not wanting in a certain grandeur, especially when the great geniuses of the thirteenth century had given it the finishing touches. There has been no period when, with such poor resources, reason has proved herself so great— so much so that, at the close of this great work of synthesis and integration there stood forth an imposing and unified system claiming universal knowledge, and, as a matter of fact, embracing almost every truth to which unaided dialectic could attain."

With the age of St. Thomas the deductive theology had attained its apogee. And there we had thought in our ignorance that Roman theology was satisfied to remain. How often we had writhed under the reproach, or smiled at it, as our mood might be, that the boasted learning of our Universities was the senseless confusion into which the retrograde modern mind was doomed to fall! Besides, if we could have remained in doubt about the official attitude of the Roman Church upon this matter, we had only to recall the encyclical *Æterni Patris* and the pious efforts of Louvain and of Rome to revive the influence of the Thomist philosophy under the imme- diate patronage of Leo XIII. But the Archbishop of Albi, at least, does not regard Thomism as the be-all and end-all of theological science. "At the very moment of its completion," he says, "the work lay open to

suspicion—*On se prit à douter d'elle.*" Discoveries were
added to discoveries. Nature revealed herself to the
Roger Bacons, the Galileos, the Gassendis. Ancient
thought awoke as the monks deciphered palimpsests
and the Turks rolled back the East upon the West. The
framework of the school proved too narrow for all these
new additions. It revealed the artificial element—*la
part d'artifice*—which lay concealed within its structure.
Then began a kind of inventory, an immense work of
analytical revision analogous to that essayed by Greece
after the great theological syntheses of Hesiod and
Epimenides. The object of knowledge split into its
fractional elements. From the womb of universal *science*
one by one *the sciences* were born, as experience and
analysis, henceforward masters of every avenue of the
mind, distinguished their elements. Analysis had not
merely established itself as a scientific method. It had
produced what Mgr. Mignot calls a "formal segmenta-
tion" of knowledge. Each separate science was constituted by the determination of its object and the
definite realization of its method. Thus, as Comte
indicated, the sciences came to range themselves in a
natural hierarchy. Those whose subject-matter was
more obstinate and complex became dependent for their
development upon the progress of those which were
simpler, "*comme dans un arbre immense les rameaux
touffus et les fleurs délicates dépendent des racines vigoureuses
et du tronc noueux.*"

Now theology, if it is to be related at all to the growth
of human knowledge, and without such relation it can
make no appeal to thoughtful men, must take account

of—more, must submit itself to—the conditions of that growth as they are established in our time. And so—

" *La théologie qui était au point de départ de la science déductive, ne peut être qu'au point d'arrivée de la science analytique.*"

The facts with which religion deals, the facts of revelation, are exactly the most complex and elusive with which human knowledge has to grapple. In one sense, indeed, they are beyond the pursuit of mere rational methods. They are assertions of the heart and the will under the impulses of Divine grace. Yet they, too, must be translated into human language, they must be localized in time and space, they must be determined in their relations with the other objects of human knowledge. And this can be done only by the aid of the critical sciences of history, philology, exegesis. The task which the modern theologian must set himself is, therefore, twofold—that of critical information and that of dogmatic interpretation. He must disentangle the facts of the Gospel with their preparation and development. He must fix the letter and the exact meaning of the texts, whether Biblical, Patristic, or Conciliar, in which the kernel of religious truth is contained. This is the task of positive theology, that branch of sacred science which has had in our day such a remarkable development corresponding to the preponderance in secular learning of critical over speculative studies. It is only when the task of positive theology is completed, or at least only when such results as it can hope to attain at any single period have actually been reached, that the field is open for speculative theology, for the co-ordination of results, the welding of them into an intelligible whole.

With this vigorous contention of Mgr. Mignot, that theology, exactly because it is a living science and in so far as it is really alive in any particular age, must be progressive, Mr. Hogan is most heartily in accord. He, too, claims that history and psychology are the essential instruments of the modern interpreter of the faith, and even the most useful weapons which its sincere defender can handle. On the one hand, they justify and strengthen some of the most essential articles of the faith. On the other, they expose the weakness of beliefs which were once considered as inevitable deductions of the faith, but have now proved to be its greatest stumbling-blocks. On the one hand, De Rossi has, in the fine phrase of Mr. Hogan, "exhumed almost every article of the Catholic creed" from the Roman Catacombs. On the other, the deductive *aberglaube* of the schools has been forced to disappear by the mere realization that the deductive method, if its use in this region could be justified at all, had been forced to the point of wanton abuse. Mr. Hogan recalls, and does a service in recalling, what the middle-age theologians had established as almost of the essence of revelation. In all that refers to the angels it seems as if nothing was unknown to them. There are great folios in which may be learned everything that relates to the celestial beings—their organisation, action, powers, functions, relations with one another, with the human race, and with the entire creation. The history of creation is narrated with a wealth of detail which no one would dare to permit himself nowadays. Our

theologians described the state of innocence as if they
had been there themselves, explaining what Adam knew
and did not know, how long he lived in the terrestrial
Paradise, what his life would have been if he had never
fallen, etc. And as with the origins, so with the ultimate
destiny of the human race. Their gaze penetrated even
into heaven, so that they could describe the life of the
saints in glory. They recounted with frightful details the
sufferings of the reprobate, assigned the place occupied
by hell, and calculated mathematically its form and
dimensions. In a word, of all the innumerable questions
which the mind of man has put to itself throughout the
ages with reference to God, to the world, or to man himself, there is none that the theologians have not discussed
and attempted to resolve with an assurance beside which
that of the modern *savant* is modesty itself.

Of course, it goes without saying that Mgr. Mignot and
Mr. Hogan attach the greatest importance to the
traditional element in theology. Is not, indeed, the
Christian tradition, of which the Bible is but one, if the
most important, element, itself the revelation ? But
revelation is a Divine deposit given in terms of human
language and knowledge. And, as we have seen,
the function of theology is, on the one hand, to
modify and adapt to changing conditions of knowledge
and habits of thought the human envelope of the faith,
and, on the other, to penetrate more profoundly the
significance of the faith itself. As the science, therefore,
whose function it is progressively to interpret the revealed
facts of religion, theology owes no more and no less
homage to tradition than does any other science. It is

the duty of every science to preserve all the truth that has been already acquired in the area of its inquiry, though it may be that the most effective way to preserve that truth will consist in disentangling it from imperfect statements in the past and in providing it with a more adequate statement in the present. So theology, by the very fact of its loyalty to tradition, is the more surely pledged to progress. Its seeming contradictions may be but the highest evidence of its loyalty to and its faith in the truth. Mgr. Mignot gives a striking instance of such apparent contradiction. In the earliest volume of the "Cursus Scripturæ Sacræ," a kind of French Encyclopædia Biblica, Père Cornely devoted 150 pages to proving the authenticity, integrity, and Mosaic authorship of the Pentateuch. In the later volumes of the very same work, Père de Hummelauer devotes just as many to the proof that the Pentateuch was the work neither of one man nor of one period, but of several centuries. Behind both views lies the same faith in the Divine truth which lies embedded in the Sacred Tradition. It is a parable of the permanent and the non-permanent in religious truth.

The sum of the matter lies in some words of Mr. Hogan's, which it is worth while to quote textually :—

" Divine truth as we find it in the teaching of the Church and the schools, wears a robe of human origin which serves at once to reveal and to conceal the reality. It presents itself to us in the Bible enveloped frequently in the most diverse Oriental metaphors. We encounter it in the Fathers, draped in the mantle of Greek philosophy. It appears anew in the schools of the

Middle Age, beneath the armour of Aristotelian dialectic. But none of these vestments is essentially necessary to it. They are only the variable accidents which reveal the hidden substance. To reach to the substance itself ; to contemplate the reality as closely as possible, shorn of every metaphor, freed from everything which is system only ; to remove the anthropomorphic images in which men have accustomed themselves to clothe God and all that is divine ; to contemplate the mysteries of the Faith apart from the terminology of the schools, as often embarrassing as useful—such is the first result of an earnest and serious study of Christian doctrine."

This is the leaven which is working in the Catholic theology of France—working through reviews, through the new Catholic Universities, through the activity and the faith of all the most thoughtful among the younger clergy. It promises surely a reconciliation near at hand between the too long alienated mind of France and its religious faith. It is in itself the beginning of that reconciliation. For the leaders of this movement at least are good Catholics who hold themselves indebted at every point to the intellectual gains of modern thought with its distinctive methods. In a Church and among a people like our own which, with whatever hesitations and compromises, have consistently believed in the compatibility of religious faith and progressive knowledge, this movement will surely be hailed with unaffected delight and followed with sympathetic confidence.

CHAPTER III

THE theological crisis in the Church of France is becoming *February* 18, more acute every day. It is almost ten years since the   1903 Abbé Loisy was virtually forced to resign his chair of Sacred Scripture at the Catholic Institute of Paris, and hastened to make his submission to the directions given by the Holy Father in the Encyclical *Providentissimus Deus*. During those ten years he has pursued his studies in lonely retirement at Bellevue, publishing their results in the " Revue d'Histoire et de Littérature Religieuses," writing under various pseudonyms in the more widely-read clerical reviews, and in these later years lecturing at the École des Hautes Études to audiences almost as large and as representative as those which throng the lecture-hall of Harnack at Berlin. Now once more the liberal movement has been struck at in the person of the frail hermit of Bellevue. Cardinal Richard, who continues the reactionary policy of his predecessor, Cardinal Guibert, has condemned Loisy's latest book and forbidden the reading of it to the faithful of his diocese on the ground that it is likely " seriously to disturb their faith in the fundamental dogmas of Catholic teaching." Loisy has himself been summoned to Rome, and it is hoped that the raw haste with which he has been condemned at Paris may prove his best safeguard from formal condemnation at the hands of the central authority.

45

But before speaking of Loisy's book, it may be well to refer to the work of the Abbé Houtin, which is said to have provoked the present storm, and which has now fallen under the ban of Cardinal Richard and the Bishop of Angers.

It is probably not merely the success of this extraordinarily outspoken and incisive account of Biblical controversy in France during the last century that has so irritated the clerical Right. It is perhaps still more the contemptuous indifference with which its author has treated their stale criticisms and vapid denunciations. In the new edition of his book he has for all reply printed as an appendix a representative selection of these elegances of polemic. It was a crushing form of reply to select, but one not likely to soothe the irritation which the original publication of the book a little less than a year ago had caused. It is reported that the book was only saved from official condemnation last April by certain vigorous representations made to Cardinal Rampolla that such a step would certainly annoy, and might perhaps alienate, the Liberal Catholics of England, America, and Germany. Now, however, it is not likely to be saved by even such considerations. The decision of the Congregation of the Index with regard to it will be awaited with interest, not only through sympathy with its courageous author, but also in view of the forthcoming report of the Biblical Commission.

Meanwhile the grounds for a condemnation of the Abbé Houtin afforded by his book might well seem sufficiently difficult of discovery to tax even the ingenuity of a Roman Congregation. He has written what is in form a bald, passionless, at first sight almost disinterested, account of the struggles of a century in the field of Biblical controversy. From beginning to end there is not a single instance of special pleading, hardly a momentary lapse of formal self-betrayal. But the book is so artfully constructed as to reveal the real mind and intention of the author on every page. Under all its resolute show of historical frigidity it becomes a passionate protest of despair against theological chicane, an overwhelming condemnation of the ineptitude of the old guard of French theology. The conviction which has sustained M. Houtin throughout in his tone of calm and dispassionate historical analysis is that the intellectual interpretation of the Christian faith can recognize the autonomy of Biblical science, not only without fear, but with a positive confidence. Dogmatic theology can no longer develop fruitfully until, or at least except in so far as, positive or historical theology is given free scope. To dictate to history beforehand what it is to discover, what results it is to reach, is to nullify it. To be willing to learn from it and to modify traditional conceptions in the light of its conclusions, is the act of faith and courage which is required of the modern theologian. That is the position for which the Liberals among the French clergy are so obstinately contending. On the last page of his book, M. Houtin for once makes a confession of his faith, though even then under the guise of a summary of the century's struggle :—

" For all those who were not content to linger in mere fictions one fact was clear. The criticism of Scripture in France, as elsewhere, had been secularised, had become *positive*. In Germany it had for long been fettered to Hegelianism. In other countries it had been dominated by confessional beliefs or by rationalism. By degrees it had everywhere become more and more free of every system, autonomous, scientific."

And he ends by quoting some wise words of the Archbishop of Albi in his famous Toulouse discourse on the Method of Theology. Mgr. Mignot is claiming " for Catholic scholars the right of freely pursuing their studies under the safeguard of the Church " :—

" Let us also grant them," he continues, " the very human right of sometimes making a mistake. Error is one of the inevitable vicissitudes of the development of the human mind. For the scholar who is sincere it is often a roundabout way of getting at the truth. And for the Catholic scholar it has less inconvenience than for any other, for with him it can only be temporary, and commits neither theology nor the Church—which at the right moment will know how to set it right. Let us, therefore, give free discussion time to do its own work. In conducting it let us employ scientific methods only, and not those invectives or that violence which witness to a zeal for orthodoxy more worthy of knights errant than of conscientious scholars. Let no one be disturbed by seeing some of our scientific conclusions agree with opinions uttered by heterodox or non-Christian scholars. That has been called ' protestantising,' ' rationalising ' the Church. But these barbarisms will not prevent science from being one and single, certainty from imposing itself upon the human mind, and serious theology from welcoming every truth whencesoever it may come."

M. Houtin's narrative divides itself naturally into two periods, very unequal indeed in duration, but each characterised by a special interest of its own. There was first the long, gradual gestation of the problem, the period of more or less open and unfettered competition between the different schools—the ultra-traditionalist, the Conservative, and the Progressive. This period was brought to a sudden and dramatic end in October, 1893, by the famous Encyclical *Providentissimus Deus*. Since then the Progressive party has been engaged in an obstinate struggle for mere existence, relying, for the most part, upon forced and unnatural interpretations of that fatal document. Neither the decision of the Congregation of the Inquisition in favour of the authenticity of the text of the three Heavenly Witnesses, nor Leo XIII's condemnation of Americanism by his letter, *Testem Benevolentiæ*, addressed to Cardinal Gibbons, nor his encyclical to the Archbishops, Bishops, and clergy of France of September, 1899, has availed to check the boldness or lessen the influence of the critical school. On the contrary, they have served only to sharpen its ingenuity and extend its power. The moral right of the critics to carry on their campaign in favour of critical freedom depends entirely upon the view that may be taken of the meaning and scope of the infallible *magisterium* of the Roman See. On that issue the battle of the next fifty years will no doubt be waged, and on its result will depend the vitality and spiritual force of the Roman Church. Meanwhile, the practical difficulty of turning any position which Rome may have taken up does not seem great. Here is M. Houtin's incidental account of the process :—

" Never has the adage, *Rome a parlé, la cause est finie,* been more in use than during the nineteenth century. Yet it has always been a far cry from the formula to its application. Rome's pronouncement does not often assume the brief and definite form which necessitates either submission or withdrawal from the Church. The pontifical directions are as a rule set forth and glossed (*exposées et commentées*) in lengthy documents. As theological discussions present for the most part a very wide range of opinion, and as the defenders of each position include in their ranks dialecticians who are both subtle and convinced, they have no difficulty in presenting under different points of view a teaching which every unprejudiced mind would assert was exceedingly definite and exceedingly strong. Lastly, the directions of the Pope may strike counter to a current so powerful, may chance upon a set of circumstances so extraordinary, that it becomes necessary to repeat them in order that they may acquire their due effect."

Biblical criticism in France may have had a more tardy development than elsewhere ; but at least it seems to have run very much the same course and to have presented the same general character. There was the same fatuous persistency in the attempt to reconcile every fresh position of geological and palæontological science with the Biblical accounts of the Creation and the Flood which made the apologetics of the mid-century in England a nightmare of pointless theology and impossible science. M. Houtin, whose humour consists in telling the truth

pointedly, details some of the absurdities of the French
Concordistes—as, for instance, when Marcel de Serres,
the defender of the "*jours-époques*" interpretation of the
first chapter of Genesis, gravely discusses whether there
is any evidence in the Bible that the introduction of
railways in the nineteenth century had been foreseen, or
when Roselly de Lorgues finds the life of Columbus and
the destiny of the American Indians clearly foretold in
the eleventh chapter of Isaiah. After all, these are only
exaggerations of the Concordist theory, the theory that
expected to find in the Bible not only scientific teaching,
but scientific prophecy. Yet in spite of these absurdities
the critical spirit was growing. That growth could not,
perhaps, be better exemplified than by a comparison of
two addresses from the chair of Holy Scripture in the
chief seat of Catholic learning, one in the year 1867, and
the other in 1892—a comparison which M. Houtin himself
makes. In 1867 the Abbé Vollot had just been appointed
Professor of Holy Scripture at the Sorbonne—for the
Faculty of Catholic Theology was then still connected
with the University—and the subject of his discourse at
the opening of the session was, " The Rights and Duties
of Criticism with regard to the Bible." In the course of
that address—which had for preface the usual disparage-
ment of the great pioneer of French Biblical criticism
condemned by Bossuet at the end of the seventeenth
century, Richard Simon—Vollot said : " Everything has
been said, wrote La Bruyère two hundred years ago—
well, on the Bible everything has been said now." Exactly
twenty-five years after, M. Loisy, in delivering his sessional
discourse at the Catholic Institute of Paris, as its Professor

of Holy Scripture, spoke with respect of Richard Simon, and declared that " the field of exegesis is immense, varied, and even in one sense and on many points almost unexplored." That is in brief the progress of a quarter of a century. Yet this progress must be discounted by the very different treatment accorded to these two young scholars by the diocesan administration of Paris, which is in great measure the official mouthpiece of.the French Church. Vollot was until his early death petted and approved. Loisy was deprived of his chair, and has been ever since the victim of a studied neglect.

The total impression left by M. Houtin's book resolves itself into the establishment of a principle and the convincing evidence of a fact. The principle is the necessity of freedom of speculation and research for the sane development of theological science. Freedom no doubt involves the certainty of extravagance and the possibility of error. But then error, as Bossuet said long ago, is only an imperfect apprehension of the truth ; or, as Mgr. Mignot says to-day, " *un chemin détourné qui conduit souvent à la vérité*." And if the atmosphere of intellectual freedom seems at first sight to foster extravagance, it also most surely kills it. The fact to which M. Houtin's narrative witnesses is that it is hard for a Roman theologian to assert and secure that freedom. It is not, of course, that there is any reality in the Protestant bugbear of an essentially persecuting spirit in the Roman Church, of a kind of love of persecution for its own sake. It is that Roman theology is dominated by a mentality of the thirteenth and fourteenth centuries, which is simply unable to meet or even to understand the living challenge

of modern theological problems. Over and over again
M. Houtin makes us feel the fatal effect of the Scriptural
decrees of the Tridentine and Vatican Councils and of the
Papal letters and Encyclicals of the last ten years in
lowering the standard and checking even the desire of
learning among the clergy, in reproving critical sincerity
and courage wherever they existed, and in deferring
the possibility of a sane apologetic until perhaps the
modern mind shall have been completely alienated from
Christianity. He makes us feel how many golden opportunities of laying the foundations of an understanding
between theology and modern ways of thinking the
Church has thrown away by her obstinate adhesion to
mediæval positions, by her refusal to admit even the
existence of difficulties. He reminds us how Quinet was
accused of atheism because, in all good faith, he appealed
to the leaders of the Church of France to treat seriously
and to answer the difficulties raised by the book of
D. F. Strauss. He reminds us of the mere unintelligent
abuse which was almost the only answer accorded to
Renan during the whole course of his career. The
disastrous effect of this policy upon clerical learning—
disastrous it must be called in presence of an almost
universal lay scepticism—is thus humorously described
by M. Houtin. He says that at the end of the nineteenth
century—

"The clergy were so much the less drawn to occupy
themselves with the question of Biblical criticism that
they knew how intolerant was the *Évêché* of any rashness
upon this ground. Perhaps, on an average, only two
priests in twenty could be found who interested themselves

in Biblical questions. Of these one declared himself an uncompromising defender of tradition, the other as open to the new ideas. Between these two battle would often be joined at clerical meetings or conferences. Discussion would promptly degenerate into bitterness and sharp words. The traditionalist would treat his adversary as a heretic, and the other, though his antagonist might be old, perhaps very old, would end by answering him in terms but little flattering to his intelligence or his information. The others would remain dumb, embarrassed, anxious not to compromise themselves, judging the young man indeed exceedingly rash, but wishing all the same that he might be right, because they would no longer have to argue with M. Homais about Adam and the apple or Jonah and the whale."

It is not merely because M. Houtin's book has been denounced to the Index, nor, again, because it is a very careful and interesting history of a special phase of theological change, that it is well worth reading. It is still more because it succeeds in being besides a transcript from life. As such it may often make the English reader feel, for himself and his Church, " *De nobis fabula*."

CHAPTER IV

" L'ÉVANGILE ET L'ÉGLISE "

On January 17th, 1903, the Cardinal Archbishop of February 25, 1903 Paris condemned M. Loisy's latest book, " L'Évangile et l'Église," a reply to Harnack's " Das Wesen des Christenthums," on the following grounds :—

" It is calculated seriously to disturb the belief of the faithful in the fundamental dogmas of Catholic teaching, notably the authority of the Scriptures and of Tradition, the Divinity of Jesus Christ, His infallible knowledge, the redemption wrought by His death, His resurrection, the Eucharist, the Divine institution of the Episcopate and of the Sovereign Pontificate."

On February 7th the *Semaine Religieuse* of the diocese of Paris published the following official notice :—

" M. Loisy has addressed a letter to his Eminence in which he states that he has stopped the publication of the second edition of his book which was just about to appear, that he yields before the judgment which has been given, and that he condemns all the errors which may have been drawn from his work. His Eminence, delighted at this step taken by the Abbé Loisy, has expressed to him his entire satisfaction with it."

Thus Loisy has made formal submission to his Diocesan, and final judgment on his book must rest with the new Biblical Commission, which, it is said, will become a permanent body, and replace the Congregation of the

Inquisition in deciding upon the orthodoxy of all works on Biblical questions.

M. Loisy has hitherto been known mainly as a scholar, so revolutionary as often to outstrip his German masters. In his latest book he appears as an apologist more revolutionary still. Yet there are two things which must impress themselves upon every one who knows his work— the sincerity of his devotion to truth, and the sincerity of his devotion to the Roman Church. He is a man endowed with most of the gifts of the really great scholar— patience, teachableness, and a rare intellectual sincerity. He is unwearied in his attempt to disentangle the facts from the documents which he handles, he keeps his mind open to receive their full and just impression, and he passes fearlessly to the conclusions which they seem to him to impose. He is not a revolutionary for the sake of being such, but because the facts as he finds them leave him no other alternative. But this is after all only the superficial activity of the man. Behind it lies a deep humble religious nature, and one which you feel has received its most intimate quality from the Roman Church, and can never be at home elsewhere.

Apart from this view of the man, it is impossible to understand his work or to state its results with any justice to himself. It is a commonplace to say that the present position of religious thought and theological speculation is transitional. But, perhaps, it is not so generally recognized what the nature of that transition is. It may, perhaps, be roughly described as a tendency to close the long period of divorce between the natural and the supernatural, to find the supernatural within the natural. For many theologians this tendency is an influence which either unconsciously colours their thought or goads them into conscious opposition. For more it leads to all kinds of compromises with traditional teaching. Loisy, perhaps more than any theologian of England or Germany, has yielded to its uncompromising logic. For him religion is in its substance and spirit divine. In its form it is always and everywhere human. It must be so, for it is not a system imposed upon an abstract humanity which does not exist, but a life infused into actual men, and in them obeying the laws of their natural growth and development. Every outward manifestation of religion—worship, dogma, government, embodiment in a redemptive society—has indeed a Divine substance, but is relative to and conditioned by temporary needs and circumstances. Therefore each of these manifestations has its own history, is always changing, and must always be changing because it is an expression of life. Worship is the expression of the religious aspirations of actual men, and changes as their religious needs change. Dogma is the interpretation of religious facts by actual men, and must change with the changing intellectual conditions which determine their apprehension of those facts. The significance of dogma is not absolute but relative :—

" The Church does not require faith in its formulas as the adequate expression of absolute truth, but presents them as the least imperfect expression which is morally possible. It asks that they should be respected according to their quality, that the faith should be sought in them, that they should be used for the transmission of that faith. The formularies of the Church are the auxiliary of faith, the guiding line of religious thought. They cannot be the integral object of this thought, since that object is God Himself, the Christ and His work. Each man appropriates the object as best he can, with the help of the formulary. As all souls and intelligences differ from one another, the shades of belief are also of an infinite variety under the one direction (*la direction unique*) of the Church and in the unity of its symbol. The continuous evolution of doctrine is the result of the effort of individuals in proportion as their activity reacts upon the general activity, and it is individuals that, thinking with the Church, think also for it."

Similarly the government of the Church has endured continual change under the immediate pressure of outward circumstances, but really in obedience to the higher necessity of preserving the Gospel, which could not have been preserved without such change. In a few masterly paragraphs Loisy has written the history of that development as he sees it. The Christian society of the first century consisted of a number of autonomous Churches, each governed by a committee of its elder members, by the *Presbyterium* rather than by individual presbyters. The condition of the life of the societies was the development of an organ of authority, however rudimentary. This College of Presbyters would naturally speak and act through some one of its individual members, who would thus gain a special prominence and even official eminence among his fellows. Under the stress of resistance to the Gnostic heresies, the value of an authority concentrated in one individual was demonstrated, and so that authority emerged from the struggle endowed with a definite *prestige.* The monarchical episcopate had been formed. But from the first there had been working in the Christian communities an instinctive feeling towards unity as the guarantee of a fuller and more durable life. Alike from its political importance as the centre of the Empire, and from the fact, due to that importance, that the greatest of the Apostles, St. Peter and St. Paul, had been led to make it the centre of Evangelical activity, Rome was marked out as the natural organ by which this feeling towards unity might express itself in fact, the natural point of concentration of the Christian communities into the Church. True, the Church of Rome was one of those in which the effective power of the Presbyteral College continued longest, in which the evolution of the monarchical episcopate was most tardy and gradual. True, also, that it was far from the thought of the great Apostles " that they were bequeathing at their death a master to Cæsar, or even giving to the Church a supreme head." But that is only one proof the more how little all this development grew out of any deliberate intention and purpose in a human mind, how entirely out of the stress of that living force in the Church whose one purpose was to preserve the Gospel under different circumstances and in face of ever-varying necessities. The unity which Rome thus established was, again, not a constant, but a growing thing, and, again, grew out of actual vital necessities. At first, she preserved unity by serving as a type to other Churches of teaching, organization, and discipline. But gradually she was forced into legislating, or rather into forming a constitution for the whole Church as one. It is necessary

again to quote M. Loisy in order to render his thought
adequately :—

" It was necessary that the Church should become a
government or cease to exist. But government in a
Church which is one and universal is inconceivable
without a central authority. An ideal centre without
real power, such as St. Cyprian conceived, would have
been useless. Differences on important questions had
to be settled somewhere. Partial councils (*les conciles
particuliers*) could not acquire a sufficient *prestige*.
General councils could never have been more than an
extraordinary tribunal, and experience proved that these
assemblies were not without very great inconvenience.
The superior and permanent tribunal to which all major
causes might naturally be referred, and whose mission
it was to provide a definite settlement of all conflicts,
could only be found in the Church which was Apostolic
above all others, which had the traditions of Peter and
Paul, and whose chiefs no longer hesitated to style
themselves successors of the Prince of the Apostles."

A further stage in the development of government in
the Roman Church was reached when, after centuries of
illusion, it was at last realised that the ancient order of
the Roman Imperium had vanished, that Europe was a
chaos. Then the Roman Church found herself intrusted
with the charge of educating the West, of kneading it
into a manageable unity through the Spirit of the
Gospel. She founded the middle-age Christian Republic
of the West, she became the head of the Christian
Confederation :—

" In that confusion, which she had to dominate in

order not herself to disappear, the Church kept on growing and transforming herself. She grew in order to endure, because the changes which were being wrought in her were the very condition of her existence. The great temporal position of the Popes during the twelfth and thirteenth centuries was only the guarantee of their independence in the spiritual order. And in that order the Popes had to be what they were, what they had become, in order that the Church might still be the Church, might not cease to be Christianity and the religion of Jesus."

And M. Loisy concludes his history of Church government with just a hint of his view of its future :—

" The Pope remains the father of the faithful and the head of the Churches." (The expression is significant.) " We may foresee that his action will never again take the form it took in the middle ages. But this power will always be needed for the preservation of the Church and for the preservation of the Gospel in the Church."

There is only one feature of religion which for M. Loisy is constant, the necessity of its embodiment in a visible society, and that is constant only because such embodiment is a constant condition of life. It is only in an organized society that religion can enter into the lives of actual men and through them grow into all its wealth of dogma and worship. It is only in an organized society that the life, the spirit, of the Gospel could have grown as it had to do if it was to remain life. But what in Loisy's view is this Gospel ? Has it any absolute form ? Has it ever expressed itself in a form which is valid for all times and places, for all souls and circumstances ?

Loisy's answer is—No. The only element of the Gospel which is absolute is its life, its soul, and that life of the Gospel was communicated to men through the Risen Christ. But his great controversy with Harnack arises out of what he describes as the arbitrary attempt of the latter to single out some portion of our Lord's teaching as of absolute value. It will be remembered that Harnack tried to distinguish between the traditional and the personal elements in the teaching of Jesus, and that he assigned to what he held to be the latter an absolute and eternal religious value, described it as the essence of Christianity. Loisy will have none of this. The teaching of Jesus is all traditional. Where is the element in that teaching which cannot be traced to tradition ? Not the belief in God as the Father, which Harnack selects, for that was held and taught by the Hebrew prophets. Not the belief in the coming Kingdom, for that, too, was the main religious heritage of Judaism. Not the certainty of eternal life, which Harnack traces solely to faith in the Risen Christ, for Plato, the religion of the Persians, and post-exilian Judaism had surely all contributed to the formation of that certainty. Not even the belief in the Divine Sonship, which Harnack (relying upon a passage common to the Gospels of St. Matthew and St. Luke— " No man knoweth the Son, but the Father ; neither knoweth any man the Father, save the Son, and he to whomsoever the Son will reveal Him ") claims as the peculiar consciousness of Jesus, though felt and known by Him as a moral relation rather than as a metaphysical identity. But Loisy, while insisting that the relation between the Father and the Son here asserted is metaphysical, refuses to accept the text as a genuine saying of Jesus, and insists that it is an interpretation, akin to the theology of the Johannine Gospel, which is due to the generation in which the Evangelical tradition was reduced to its present form. As to the undoubted claim of Jesus to Divine Sonship, he sees no reason as an historian to believe that it was other than His belief that He was Messiah :—

"*Jésus se dit fils unique de Dieu dans la mesure où il s'avoue Messie. L'historien en conclura, hypothétiquement, qu'il se croyait fils de Dieu depuis qu'il se croyait Messie.*"

And, equally, the teaching of Jesus is all relative. No part of it in the form in which it was given holds good for all time, because it was not meant for all time. It was meant for actual men. If it had not been so meant and so adapted, it would never have had any effect, it would have perished still-born. Religion is life, and, no matter by whom communicated as mere teaching, must conform to the conditions of life. Nor, again, will Loisy have anything to do with those who hold the accommodation theory—the theory that Jesus consciously accommodated His teaching to the intelligence and the existing religious belief of His time. " Jesus spoke in order to say what He thought true without the least regard to our categories of absolute and relative." The truth is that the teaching of Jesus all centred about the proclamation of the great hope—" *la grande espérance.*" That is the real " essence of Christianity," and that had been drawn from the heart of Judaism to be transfigured in the life of the Risen Christ into a fuller religious force propagating itself in its own way by its own inherent energy. The actual form of that hope as Jesus taught it and conceived it had already changed within the lifetime of some of His apostles. But such change was again the very condition of its life :—

" It was neither possible nor would it have served any useful purpose that the future of the Church should be revealed by Jesus to His disciples. The thought that Jesus bequeathed to them was the necessity of continuing to desire, to prepare, to expect, to realise the kingdom of God. The perspective of the kingdom has been widened and modified, that of its definite arrival has receded, but the aim of the Gospel has remained the aim of the Church."

The Cardinal who is reported to have said that if Loisy's ideas prevailed the Church would be revolutionised was not far wrong. Nor would the revolution be confined to the Church of Rome. This book is a reply to Harnack, but it answers him by convicting him of an impossible compromise with orthodoxy. It is certainly by strangely different ways that the reunion of Christendom is being sought after on the Continent of Europe and at home. If it is true that Loisy is not to be condemned by Rome (and it is well known that he has powerful friends and protectors), then the words of the Abbé Marcel Hébert may have a more immediate meaning than one thinks. " A day will come when Catholicism also will make its act of Protestantism, and then there will be an end of the latter "—and, perhaps we may add, a beginning of the former.

CHAPTER V

"AUTOUR D'UN PETIT LIVRE"

"L'ÉVANGILE ET L'ÉGLISE" was a noteworthy book. *December 2,* The amplification of it which M. Loisy has just given us *1903* in his "Autour d'un Petit Livre" is still more noteworthy. In it he has defined his method, one would say beyond the possibility of misunderstanding, and applied it in new and important directions. The new work consists of a series of seven letters addressed to eminent French Churchmen. The names of the *destinataires* are not given, but by anyone who knows even a little of the contemporary Church of France most of them will be easily recognized. The Cardinal, for instance, to whom the letter on the Biblical question is addressed, is obviously Cardinal Perraud, Bishop of Autun. The letter on the Criticism of the Gospels, addressed to a Bishop, is as evidently a reply to the attack upon M. Loisy's former book from the pen of Mgr. Le Camus, Bishop of La Rochelle. And equally there need be no hesitation about the recognition of Mgr. Mignot, Archbishop of Albi, M. Loisy's closest theological ally, in the friendly prelate to whom the essay on the Divinity of Jesus Christ is communicated. Internal evidence points to the Abbé Félix Klein as the recipient of the fifth letter, that which deals with the foundation and authority of the Church, and to M. François Thureau-Dangin, the learned son of the Academician and historian of English Tractarianism, as the youthful scholar to whom the letter on the origin and authority of dogma is addressed. The first letter and the last, the one a further elucidation of the purpose of " L'Évangile et l'Église," the other a critical examination of the institution of the Sacraments, are addressed respectively to a " Curé Doyen," and a " Supérieur de Séminaire," whom the present writer cannot venture to identify.

The identification of these names is no mere impertinence of an irrelevant curiosity. It is, on the contrary, a most interesting guide to the variety of tone which marks the different letters. With his friends Mgr. Mignot, M. Klein, and M. Thureau-Dangin, M. Loisy expands in an easy and luminous exposition of his theme, confident of understanding and sympathy. But in the letters to the Bishops of Autun and La Rochelle there is something of the note of conflict which gives them a special piquancy and force. It is unnecessary to say that M. Loisy's frankness is always good-tempered and urbane. But it is also fearless. It is the unhesitating frankness of the scholar who is sure of his scholarship and of the believer who is sure of his faith.

M. Loisy has been accused by the perverse or otiose unintelligence of his critics of denying almost every article of the Christian faith. This book is a demonstration for the reader of good faith that M. Loisy affirms every Christian belief with a personal certainty which has been reached through a fresh intellectual appreciation of its contents, an appreciation determined by the knowledge and the mental habit of our time. It is indeed just his sympathy with the difficulties in the way of faith created

by the rift between modern ways of thinking and the
traditional presentation of Christian beliefs that will not
allow him to play the part of the theological ostrich or to
discuss theological questions *in camerâ* :—

" It is not assuredly in France," as he well says, " since
the time of Renan that a non-ecclesiastical reader is
likely to be perturbed by the discussion of the thorniest
questions. Have not all those educated laymen who,
baptised and brought up in the Catholic Church, leave
it as soon as they have reached the age of manhood,
decided for themselves—and alas ! all too hastily—the
problems of the Christ and of God, because our religious
teaching appears to them conceived in a spirit of hostility
to science and history ? Is it not already to have done
much for them, just to have shown that we are not
unaware of the nature of their difficulties, that we
appreciate their intellectual sensitiveness, that we are
thinking of them and desire to clear the way for their
return to the fold ? "

And elsewhere, in discussing the Christological problem,
he says, with a true intelligence of actual needs :—

" If we keep silence upon this serious question, if we
confine ourselves to a recitation of the traditional formula,
we are abandoning to doubt and unbelief numbers of
souls who do not even know that they have a right, in
company with the Church and with us, to seek for a better
understanding of the Gospel."

It may be well to select M. Loisy's treatment of this
very problem for a somewhat detailed examination both
on account of its own intrinsic importance and as an
instance of his general conception of dogma and his

method of handling it. Many friendly critics of M. Loisy outside the Roman Church, and many hostile critics within it, have professed themselves unable to understand his position as at once an obedient son of the Church and a scholar holding the most advanced critical positions on Biblical and dogmatic questions. For M. Loisy himself the incompatibility does not exist. On the contrary, it is of the very essence of Catholicism to believe in what I may call the progressive permanence, the permanence through an unending development, of the faith of Christendom. The object of the Christian faith is one and permanent. That object is realised progressively, though always inadequately, in the religious experience of Christendom. It is formulated progressively, but with even less adequacy, in the intellectual definitions of the Christian faith. A dogma is the definition of a particular phase of the religious experience of Christendom which is authorised by the Church at a particular moment of its history. All these definitions or formulas have only a provisional and relative value. They are vehicles of the truth. They exist to stimulate the faith in individual souls, to help it to grow to an ever fuller consciousness of itself. If it were otherwise, there would be no need of the living direction of the Church. The Pope and the Councils would have become a mere cumbering superfluity. It would be necessary only, in order to ascertain the adequate statement of the faith, to provide one's self with a complete record of past decisions of Councils or of Popes. It would be to apply to the completed conciliar and patristic tradition the old Protestant view of the Bible as an absolute rule of

faith. But nothing, M. Loisy holds, is more opposed to
the real spirit of Catholicism, as nothing is more harmful
to the human mind, than the worship of formulas. The
real rule of faith ought to be as living as faith itself. And
such a rule can be found only in revelation, as from age
to age it is actually interpreted by the living Church and
put to the proof in the living souls that make the Church.
For the interpretation which is a rule of faith at any
moment is just as much the result of the religious
experience of the Church's children as it is her own
authoritative form of explanation. Indeed, the latter
depends upon the former. It is the *ecclesia discens* that
provides for the constitution of the *ecclesia docens*. And
there is no finality for the rule of faith. So long as the
human mind grows, the intellectual expression of that
which has been spiritually discerned will widen.

Now all this (M. Loisy holds) applies to the growth of
Christological as of all other dogmas. The starting-point
of Christian faith is that Christ is God. A Christian is
just one whose religious experience is mediated to him
through that initial belief. But that faith, to which the
whole history of Christianity has been a growing witness,
has been intellectually appreciated by men of different
generations in very different ways. At the present
moment the great claim upon the Church is that she
should once more make real to the modern world what
she means by the very terms Christ and God. She is at
present using definitions which were framed in another
intellectual language, another intellectual atmosphere,
than ours. For us they are meaningless when they are
not misleading. Those who keep the faith of Christendom,

the faith that Christ is God, keep it in spite of the formulas. Many of those who lose it, lose it because of the unintelligibility of the formulas, and because they believe that the formulas as they stand are regarded by the Church as an absolute statement of truth. The vital necessity of the moment is a translation of the formulas into terms of actual thought. To that end two things will be helpful—first, a history of the growth of interpretation in the past, and secondly, an analysis, in the light of modern knowledge, of the religious ideas involved. The former task M. Loisy has undertaken and carried through with considerable minuteness. He has indicated the main lines on which the latter must proceed. The former is historical, the latter mainly philosophical.

The duty of the historian is to ascertain facts and so to establish the living reality to which the record that he may be examining bears witness. The counsel of perfection for the historian is to avoid at all costs the importing of the ideas of a later time into the record of an earlier. Like all counsels of perfection, it is naturally difficult of complete fulfilment. But at least the effort to give effect to it must be made if we would arrive at the truth or anything near the truth. Now M. Loisy accuses the traditional Christian theologian of having conspicuously neglected this counsel in his examination of the Gospel records. He has deliberately read into them something which the historian cannot possibly find there. M. Loisy refuses to follow his example. For instance, the orthodox theology has insisted on ascribing to the Jesus of history a full consciousness of His Divine nature as it was affirmed in the developed speculation of fourth or fifth century

Councils—that is to say, of His consubstantiality with the Father. For M. Loisy that speculation was thoroughly justified. It preserved, as no other statement at that time could have done, the essential faith of Christendom, the faith in Christ as God. But it *was* speculation. It in no way corresponded with the psychological reality of the consciousness of Jesus. It is impossible for the historian to say what the full reality of that consciousness was. But, at least, it is impossible to ask the historian to assert that it coincided exactly with a phase of human speculation determined by fourth-century Hellenistic philosophy, even though we believe that the results of that speculation were the most adequate interpretation of the Christian faith that was then possible, and believe further that it was guided to those results, in common with all other sincere human thought, by the Divine Spirit working through the human intellect. All that the historian can assert of the self-consciousness of Jesus is what he finds by the witness of the synoptic record that Jesus asserts about Himself. And that is that He was the Messiah announced by Jewish prophecy. It is true, indeed, that the conception of the Messiah, which the synoptic tradition ascribes to Jesus, was in one important point a development of the contemporary Jewish conception. The unique relation of the Messiah to Israel persists in the synoptic account of the witness of Jesus to Himself, but the strictly national element in that relation is absorbed into and lost sight of in a moral relation. Here is the germ of that universal redemptive relation of Jesus to humanity, on which the faith of Christendom seized, under the guidance of the

Spirit, and out of which all later Christology naturally grew. In other words, what M. Loisy would insist upon is that the perception that Christ was God was a perception of faith. That perception was, of course, the perception of a real fact, of the supreme religious fact. But its actual realization in the Christian consciousness was the gradual result of difficulties which it had to meet and overcome, and the business of the historian is to disengage the stages and the process of its growth. The first test which this faith had to encounter was the death of Jesus. It met it victoriously by the belief in the Resurrection, a belief which, as M. Loisy holds, the Synoptists show to have been a belief in the immortal life of the Crucified " still more than in the initial fact which is suggested to our minds by the word resurrection. The apostolic preaching did not insist upon the circumstances of this resurrection, but upon the existence of the Risen One."

In support of his view that the belief in the Resurrection was a great act of faith rather than the result of mere sensible evidence, M. Loisy reminds us that the Gospel tradition preserves the memory of doubts which had arisen at the very time of the recorded appearances of the Risen Lord, and also witnesses to the conscious effort of the faith to justify itself by an appeal to the prophetic promises of the Old Testament. At any rate the faith of Christendom had taken the first step in its upward progress. Out of the simple Messianic idea had grown the faith in the immortal life of the Risen Lord. Faith in Jesus as the Christ had victoriously met its first test. The growth of Christology had begun. As a historian M. Loisy details the history of this growth, the deepening consciousness of Christendom of the content and implications of its faith, the historical circumstances which necessitated each stage in the advance. First within the pages of the New Testament he exposes the occasion and the character of the Christology of St. Paul, of that of the Epistle to the Hebrews, of that of the Fourth Gospel. Beyond the limits of the New Testament he continues the history until the completed Christology of the fifth century is reached.

But the objection will at once be raised that between the highly developed Christology of Chalcedon and the synoptic witness to the self-consciousness ot Jesus there is a great gulf fixed, that they do not testify to the same fact. That is just what M. Loisy will not admit. For, first of all, let it be remembered what this Christology was. It was an attempt to define not what Jesus taught about Himself, but what Jesus was for the Christian consciousness. The definitions were the most adequate representation that was possible of what Jesus was, in the circumstances and under the conditions of their origin. But between them and the actual consciousness of Jesus there was all the difference that always separates the abstract from the real. What was the actual consciousness of Himself which Jesus possessed the historian, of course, cannot completely determine. " The feeling which Jesus had of His union with God is above all definition." But, at least, the tradition bears witness to His consciousness of such a union, in testifying to His belief in Himself as the Messiah. The *substance* of His self-consciousness is, therefore, one with the consciousness

of Christendom about Him which found expression in
the fully developed speculative Christology of the fifth
century.

But that Christology M. Loisy proclaims to be no longer
adequate. It was conceived in terms of a philosophy
which no longer holds. It depended upon a view of God
which conceived of Him as apart from the world, on a
view of the world which conceived of it as apart from
God. The traditional theory of the Incarnation was
framed to fit in with this conception of a transcendent
God desiring to establish relations with a world which
was separated from Him. The Word was the intermediary of creation, an emanation from God towards the
world. Such theories have no longer any meaning for
us. The "spatial transcendence" theory, as Père
Laberthonnière has aptly called it, must be abandoned
because it no longer helps us to conceive of God. Every
acquisition of knowledge in our time forces us, if we
would retain a vital doctrine of God, to conceive of Him
as immanent in the world and in man, needing no intermediary in order to act upon and in both. Physical
science is forcing us to a fresh analysis of the religious
idea of creation which will provide for God's immediate
activity in the world of nature. History is forcing us to
a fresh analysis of the idea of revelation which will
provide for God's immediate activity in the total spiritual
development of human society. Psychology is forcing
us to a fresh analysis of the idea of redemption which will
provide for God's moral action in the development of the
individual soul. Out of this threefold analysis will issue
a new and fruitful realization of God as operant in the

world and in man. For the religious mind the rationalism which conceives of a purely transcendent God and of a purely human Christ will become unmeaning and impossible. The Christian faith that Christ is God will be established through conceptions which the modern mind can appreciate.

This is a most imperfect summary of a stimulating fragment of a stimulating book. Some, who will think it dangerous and revolutionary, may perhaps be impressed by the fact that M. Loisy does not stand alone—that he has at least two great French prelates, one of them a considerable theologian, behind him ; that he is followed by a growing band of devout thinkers among the Catholic clergy and educated laity of France, Italy, Germany, America, and England. Let them remember, too, that if M. Loisy is known as a daring and original thinker, he is known equally as a devout and humble soul. His work is important. It must be reckoned with.

CHAPTER VI

MR. INGE AND M. LOISY

December,
1904 IT was with a feeling of very genuine surprise that some months ago I read Mr. Inge's sermon on Liberal Catholicism in the *Guardian*. For if I had been asked to name an English theologian who would unreservedly appreciate what I had taken to be the position of M. Loisy, I should at once have named Mr. Inge. That surprise has been intensified by a reading of Mr. Inge's recently published volume of sermons.* For, all that I most admire in M. Loisy's attitude, all that seems to me most characteristic of his view of religion, is here put again and again with a force and incisiveness which are rare in theological writing. Here, for instance, is a passage which might be taken as an illuminating introduction to all that M. Loisy has written. " Our religious faith is deeper and fuller than the expressions which it finds for itself. Being in its essence Divine, faith can never fully embody itself in any human forms. It is not exactly above *Reason,* for the reason of man, as a Greek theologian said, is the throne of the Godhead, but it is above *Rationalism,* the logic of the understanding. Rationalism can neither give us religion nor deprive us of it. The relation of religious truth to other kinds of truth—a problem of immeasurable complexity—is made hardly at all clearer by either orthodox or anti-orthodox rationalism." I can hardly imagine a statement with

* " Faith and Knowledge." T. & T. Clark, Edinburgh, 1904.

76

which, as I think, M. Loisy would more heartily and in every detail agree.

But Mr. Inge is evidently sincerely convinced that M. Loisy has pronounced a permanent divorce between Faith and Reason, that he has attempted "to render faith invulnerable by separating it entirely from science." Now I think that this is a complete misunderstanding of M. Loisy's position, and I cannot help feeling that Mr. Inge has here inadvertently made M. Loisy the victim of his own persistent suspicion of the Pragmatist philosophy. The truth is that nowhere does M. Loisy distinguish between faith and science otherwise than as they are distinguished in fact. And that distinction could not be better expressed than in Mr. Inge's own words. "When religious faith is challenged to justify itself, it is almost obliged to argue and give reasons. But in reality it knows that it cannot be acquitted or condemned by the categories of the understanding : its inspiration and its energy are drawn from a deeper and a more mysterious source. It wells up from the depths of the basal personality ; its fresh springs are fed by the river of God, the eternal fountain of all life." That is to say, faith is native to the religious sense. It is the original vital perception of eternal realities, or rather, the original point of contact of the living spirit of man with their infinite and all-informing life. And that is the one supernatural moment of religion. Hardly has that supernatural conception of the religious instinct been accomplished before the birth-pangs of its release through reason into the natural world of knowledge begin to declare themselves. Faith is not fully faith till it has formed some kind of expression, however rudimentary. The supernatural is not real for us till it has mingled and become one with the natural. And yet if we would make clear to ourselves each moment of the process of faith, we must distinguish between the original undiluted certainty for the active spirit, and that certainty as it becomes mediated with increasing clearness by and for the mind. That is the real distinction between faith and the science which faith may use. And it is the only distinction between faith and science to which, so far as I can see, M. Loisy ever commits himself. Dogma is always for him that Divine-human fact, that vital inter-blending of the immutable Divine certainty which is immediately given to what Mr. Inge calls the religious instinct and the temporary and changing forms of know-ledge which may be required to explicate it. In every dogma there is the core of Divine truth which the religious instinct originally affirmed, and on which it continually seizes in order to sustain its life. But in it there is also the form which was originally given by the mental habit of a particular moment, and which, even when it does not change in outward appearance, is ever freshly apprehended by each slightest increase of knowledge, and even by each faintest variety of intellectual activity which is at all sincere. In short, dogma as a mere *statement* of Divine truth belongs at least in part to the natural order. Its birth, growth, decay, renewal are determined by the restless activity of the human mind. But in so far as it serves to elicit that immediate certainty of God and the heavenly order which presided at its conception, which lay behind its birth into the world of time, it is supernatural and eternal. Its conception is purely spiritual; its birth and life are partly intellectual, and must share in the variety and relativity of mental apprehension. And yet we can never separate Divine and human, natural and supernatural, *as we have to do with them*, except as elements in a process. Something like this seems to me to be the distinction which M. Loisy makes between faith and knowledge. And surely the religious life itself clamours for this distinction. Surely, too, which is more to the present purpose, Mr. Inge himself, in the passage which I have quoted, insists upon it.

But Mr. Inge did not make his charge against M. Loisy of separating faith " entirely from science " without producing his *pièce justificative*. He quotes the following passage with a confidence which is far from being justified by any support which, so far as I can see, it is likely to offer to his contention. " The principle of criticism does not permit us to formulate any conclusions of faith ; and no theological principle authorizes us to formulate conclusions of history. Historical researches only tend to prove and represent facts, which cannot be in contradiction with any dogma, precisely because they are facts." Far from proclaiming an absolute divorce between faith and science, this passage seeks to define the nature and limits of their necessary connection—a definition which is the special apologetic need of the moment. Let us see what M. Loisy says. " The principle of criticism does not permit us to formulate any conclusions of faith." The purpose of criticism is to elucidate fact. When it has contributed all it can to that end, its work is accomplished. Only if the facts as phenomenal happenings, as happenings

whose full scope and import were appreciable by
sense-experience, constituted a Divine Revelation, would
criticism have any direct dealings with their faith-value.
But the inspiration in virtue of which the religious
instinct finds a Divine Revelation in certain facts is
drawn, in Mr. Inge's words, "from a deeper and a more
mysterious source " than sense-experience. It is true
that the view of the facts might be so modified by
criticism as to leave in them no object for faith, nothing
which the religious instinct could recognize as Divine. But
it is just M. Loisy's contention that criticism has not so
affected the evangelical documents. He holds that the
distinctively Christian affirmation of the religious sense,
the belief in Christ as God, is still possible through that
presentation of the life and teaching of Jesus which the
most rigorous criticism has left us. But he also indicates
his belief that the assertions of the Christian faith are
still assured less in spite of critical negations than by
virtue of positive developments of faith itself. It is the
deepening of the content of faith, a deepening which is
moral rather than intellectual, which has enabled us to
find God in events which fit into the orderly natural
movement of history. The religious sense is growing
more inclined to find God in the perfection of man's moral
nature than in what seem to us arbitrary manifestations
of power in the order of physical nature. Criticism is so
far from having the power of formulating conclusions of
faith that, if it were to establish to-morrow the certainty
of all those events of the Gospel record which are usually
described as miraculous, it would not have added in the

slightest degree to the faith of a generation which seeks elsewhere the vision of God.

And again, M. Loisy holds that " no theological principle authorizes us to formulate conclusions of history." I cannot think that Mr. Inge would dispute the obvious justice of such a proposition. The facts of past history are beyond our manipulation. They happened in such and such a definite fashion. Not even faith, much less a particular theological principle, can be allowed to come in beforehand to confuse our perception of what the facts really were. It will be difficult enough for criticism to disentangle those facts. Its success will never be more than approximate. But at least historical criticism is the one instrument which we have at our disposal for the attainment of that end, and it must be left as free as possible to pursue it.

But it is perhaps in M. Loisy's assertion that facts " cannot be in contradiction with any dogma, precisely because they are facts," that his chief offending lies. Now here again, and indeed here especially, I would say that M. Loisy, so far from proclaiming a complete separation between faith and science, is insisting upon their consentient witness. They are indeed for him different modes of apprehension, each valid in its own sphere. But for one who believes in a Divine activity in the facts of history, and in a supreme expression of that activity in the life of Jesus of Nazareth culminating in the manifestation of His risen life as Lord and Christ, their witness must agree. It is not of course enough to assert that agreement. It cannot exist in contradiction of the reason ; it can only exist for the reason. And if M. Loisy, while admitting the results of criticism in modifying our view of the evangelical fact, simply reasserted the absolute validity of dogma in its actual form, he might justly be accused of irrationalism. But he does nothing of the kind. The only value which he attaches to dogma is the value which it has in preserving certain affirmations of the religious sense which, though they are inherent in that human reason which is in us " the throne of the Godhead," yet are logically and even vitally anterior to any rational process. It is in virtue of its essential spiritual witness that it cannot, for the religious mind, contradict facts, and exactly because they are facts through which the religious sense attains to its vision of God. But if the spirit of dogma is its power to preserve and evoke certain affirmations of the religious instinct, its form was determined by the exigencies of a definite intellectual struggle to preserve and elucidate those affirmations. Viewed from this side, dogma is little more than an interesting record of the historical fortunes of what is original and essential in Christian faith. And M. Loisy at least thinks that in this aspect dogma needs just now to be analysed anew, exactly because of our fresh gains of knowledge in the fields of physical science, history, and psychology. The whole aim of his apologetic has been to make dogma in the largest sense reasonable for the modern habit of mind. He has been condemned by Roman orthodoxy because he insisted on the necessity of distinguishing between the religious and the intellectual contents of dogma, because he held that the one was the spiritual perception of Divine realities, varying only in the measure of its vital intensity and fulness, the other, the intellectual apprehension of those realities, varying always according to the changing human modes of apprehending and expressing truth. And if he distinguishes between these, it is not because he thinks that faith as spiritual perception can dispense with some mode of intellectual apprehension and expression, but because he wishes to give that faith an intellectual translation which will be valid for current modes of thought, so that it may become a living force in this generation.

But it is in Mr. Inge's account of M. Loisy's view of the relation between the Christ and the Church that he does him most injustice. M. Loisy's view of these relations is very simple and, as it seems to me, entirely reasonable. He starts from the common Christian faith in the Catholic Church as an integral part of the faith in the Holy Spirit. But how is that faith to be justified historically ? Does the evangelical history warrant us in asserting that Jesus, during His life on earth, foresaw or forewilled the actual development of the Church in history ? Did He forewill, for instance, the primacy of Peter, or was the early preponderance of Rome in the Christian world determined, at least so far as the examination of the historian can penetrate into the sphere of causes, by purely historical circumstances ? The answer of the historian is unhesitating. He can see the dawn of the very conception of the Catholic Church in the circumstances which the first Apostles, and especially St. Paul, had to face. Equally all the later developments of the Church have their place in the orderly movement of history. But the very idea of a movement of history is an assertion of faith. It is the vision of a continuous purpose giving meaning and vital connection to isolated events, of a supreme determination of the struggles from which these events issue. And the peculiarly Christian faith is the vision of a Divine purpose which had at once its inauguration and its implicit accomplishment in the life of Jesus Christ, but which is being explicitly wrought out in the life of the Church, and will not be historically completed until that life has reached its earthly term. It is certainly the belief of M. Loisy that the Church has grown *out of* Jesus Christ, out of what He taught and consciously sought, but it is equally his belief that it must grow *into* Him, into what He essentially was. Only if Mr. Inge insists on identifying the reality of what Jesus was with His self-consciousness as man will his charge against M. Loisy have any force. The life of the Church is in some real sense an unfolding in time of the Spirit of the Risen Christ, of the fulness of the life of Jesus as it entered into its eternal victory through the grave and gate of death.

But does M. Loisy leave the impression upon his readers that this life of the Church has been expressed absolutely in any single phase of its historical development or in the whole course of that development hitherto ? Does he lay himself open to the charge of divinising the Papacy, of giving it the absolute warrant of a Divine authorship to impose its arbitrary and unchallenged rule upon the Church of God ? I cannot think how anyone who has read pages 175–186 of the " Autour d'un Petit Livre " can accuse him of so infantile a conception. Nor can I imagine how anyone, even the most convinced Protestant, can have read those pages without learning to respect and even to sympathise with the attitude of a Liberal Romanist towards the development of the idea of authority in his Church. That attitude is that authority as defined by the decrees of 1870 was the result of the instinct to preserve the ideal of Christian unity. No doubt it is open to us to maintain that that ideal was trampled upon by Rome herself in the sixteenth century, that the fact of disruption is chargeable largely to her account. Yet unity *is* a Christian ideal; it is an expression of the spirit of Christ, and it required perhaps the disaster of Christian disruption and anarchy to bring that home conclusively to the Christian conscience. If that is so, then unmistakably Rome stood thenceforward as the hope and the visible centre of the desired unity. And if unity is in fact to be restored, it will be as M. Loisy claims, in virtue of an entire change of front on the part of Rome. Authority has asserted the full measure of its claims. It can only continue to exist in discharging the full measure of its responsibilities. In establishing its claims it has forgotten its responsibilities. It has aimed at an intellectual and spiritual despotism. It has to learn that its only justification lies in its becoming the servant of all, the mediator of that true Christian unity which is essentially spiritual, and whose very existence depends upon variety of worship and intellectual interpretation, not only permitted, but cherished. Here, as elsewhere, M. Loisy is a true evangelical. He brings every development of the Church back to the judgment-seat of Christ, to the spirit of the Gospel. He demands of his Church that it shall procure " the conciliation of the rights of the

sovereign individual with those of the servant authority."
No Protestant could make a more stringent claim. The
hope of the Church's future lies for him in a return to
what he calls the "perpetual charter of the Gospel."
"The Kings of the Gentiles have lordship over them;
and they that have authority over them are called
Benefactors. But ye shall not be so; but he that is the
greater among you, let him become as the younger, and
he that is chief as he that doth serve. For whether is
greater, he that sitteth at meat, or he that serveth? Is
not he that sitteth at meat? But I am in the midst of
you as he that serveth." And he adds, "The law of the
Messianic vocation is also the law of the apostolic vocation.
Jesus served the apostles; the apostles and their successors were to be the servants of the faithful. Thanks
to the Gospel, the peoples of the modern world are coming
to understand that the only *raison d'être* of authority in
a human society is the welfare of the collectivity, i.e., of
all those who form part of that society. The *élite* which
guides is at the service of the mass which is guided. A
nation does not exist for the good of its government, but
the government exists for the good of the nation. It
would be strange if the Church, which has made this truth
prevail in the world, should in her own case deny it, or
recognise in the hierarchy a right which was not a duty
or a service towards the community."

In short, M. Loisy does not exalt the Church above
the Christ of the Gospels. The Church in which he
believes is not the Church of a particular moment, but
the Church of the Eternities, the "fulness of Him that
filleth all in all," accomplishing that fulness in time, and

accomplishing it in the midst of temporary struggle and loss, and perhaps defeat ; the Church which is growing up into the fulness of Christ exactly because and exactly in the measure that it grows out of Him, which is growing out of Him just in so far and no farther than as it is growing into Him. M. Loisy does not save the Creeds at the expense of the Gospels. He finds in both the relative expressions, each accordant to the needs and capacities of a particular time, of that " strength of the might of God which He wrought in Christ, when He raised Him from the dead and made Him to sit at His right hand in the heavenly places, and put all things in subjection under His feet, and gave Him to be head over all things to the Church, which is His body, the fulness of Him that filleth all in all." Above all, he finds in the Gospels the spirit which alone gives life to the Creeds and the Church, the spirit by which they live ideally and by which their actual life must continually be reproved, inspired, developed.

CHAPTER VII

M. DESJARDINS AND M. LOISY

December 23, 1905 A CONSIDERABLE literature has already grown up around the Affaire Loisy. It is, by the way, a piquant and instructive comment upon our ordinary literary valuations that a word, which by its origin so distinctly challenges quality, should have come to represent only the gross measure of quantity. M. Desjardins' discussion of the Affaire, at least, is considerable in the older and worthier sense. It is distinguished by an accurate and exhaustive knowledge of the facts, a sympathetic and at the same time critical intelligence of M. Loisy's position, and a studious justice in assessing the various kinds and degrees of motive which contributed to the hostile verdict of Catholic authority. M. Desjardins is careful to label himself on his title-page *un profane*, and of course with technical correctness. But the author of *Le Devoir Présent* has once again demonstrated that he is a soul naturally religious and naturally Christian. He is one of the few men in France who have at once sufficient sympathy with the world of faith and sufficient authority in the world of thought to treat so delicate a theme with much hope of success. And that he has been successful, successful in understanding his author and in challenging for him the interest of a world which is usually indifferent to theology, no one who reads this little book* is likely to deny.

* " Catholicisme et Critique." Paris, 1905.

But it will be necessary to confine ourselves here to a single point. M. Desjardins, picturing the isolation to which M. Loisy's originality condemns him, imagines the astonishment of M. Lavisse or M. Seignobos at meeting this proposition in some university thesis : " The Church may claim that, in order to be at every epoch what Jesus willed that the Society of His Friends should be, it has had to be what it has been. For in preserving itself it has been what it also needed to be in order to preserve the Gospel." Now it so happens that this passage, whatever emotion it might arouse in a French university professor, has in fact stirred, and perhaps not unnaturally, the indignant protest of many Protestant and Anglican theologians. Indeed, M. Desjardins has himself stated M. Loisy's belief upon this point in a form so absolute as might at first sight entirely justify such protests. M. Loisy believes, he says, " that this movement of the Christian Church is different in kind from all the other movements, fortuitous, or at least wavering and confused, which are registered by history. He recognizes it as a development which is constant, rectilinear, preserved from all forwandering by a hidden force which is the Spirit of God." And he adds that this thesis places M. Loisy as an interpreter of history " on a different plane from rationalist and critical historians in such a way that he appears to them as a frank apologist of Catholicism." Now, it is quite intelligible that not only to the rationalist historian but to the religious historian as well who is also an evolutionist, the establishment of such a line of demarcation as is here suggested may appear artificial and quite untenable. And it is equally intelligible that to the religious historian who, believing that the history of Christianity has been in some sense providentially safeguarded from historical risks and accidents, happens at the same time to be a non-Catholic, it may seem apposite to inquire why the Roman Church alone should be the object of such miraculous guidance, or how it can be established that such is indeed the case.

But the truth is that both these kinds of protest are premature and unnecessary. If there be a historian so rationalistic and so irrational as to regard history as mere phenomenalism, then he is certainly moving in a different plane of thought from M. Loisy, and indeed from all men who would exact some kind of order from human affairs. But M. Desjardins, by his most intelligent exposition of M. Loisy's opinions throughout this little book, is sufficient witness that the phrase which I have just quoted from him was somewhat unguarded, or at least was used only with a view to the possible exponents of historical phenomenalism. Indeed, he himself has qualified, or rather annulled, his unguarded phrase by an eloquent passage a few pages further on. If we could place ourselves at M. Loisy's point of view, he says, " sacred history would return into the main current of general history, or rather the latter would become sacred in its entirety ; the elimination of the heterogeneous in the cosmos, in history, in the conscience, would be accomplished gently and without break ; the idea of the divinity of a particular person or a particular institution would disengage itself gradually from the contradictions which it entails." That, it seems to me, is nearer M. Loisy's thought. The " hidden force which is the Spirit of God " is operating throughout the whole scheme of things. It is operating with such different degrees of effectiveness that there are whole regions of its activity in which we cannot define its method or assess its triumph or even definitely trace its course. It is only when we come to the human personality, to something within which we habitually dwell and of which we are, that we can begin not only to know its operation within that personality, but to carry of necessity the assertion of its activity beyond those confines. Now the character of its operation to which this practically universal experience testifies is twofold—its universality and its variety. It is acting throughout the whole movement of life, and yet acting uniquely in each contributory individual centre of the movement. Thus the idea of the divinity of a particular person or a particular institution, if it involves an exclusive claim to the manifestation of the Divine action in them, becomes unthinkable and, as M. Desjardins says, " enveloped in contradictions." But the same idea becomes not only thinkable but a necessity of thought when it is used to express what, from the one side, we may regard as the highest manifestation among many of this Divine force, from the other the fullest and most conscious adhesion of the human will, individual or collective, to the Divine. And this is just what M. Loisy holds about a particular institution, the Catholic Church. In a world which is still a relative and growing expression of the absolute, the Society of the Friends of Christ, the society which underneath and through all its changes and mistakes has consciously and consistently aimed at being such, is so far the most perfect collective human expression of that hidden force of all history which is the Spirit of God, is so far the divine institution *par excellence*. Will, at least, any Christian deny this, or will he refuse the hope and belief that whatever more perfect expression of that Spirit the future may hold in its womb will be in largest measure the natural and legitimate development of that institution ? Or, will any Christian deny, even if he be not himself a member of the Roman Church, that for Christendom at large the Roman Church has been the providential (in the sense of supremely adapted and therefore on the religious assumption supremely guided) depositary of those ideas by which the Spirit of Christ has lived and wrought among men, by which the Society of the Friends of Christ has endured in ideal and in fact ? It is, of course, true that for nearly four hundred years the Anglican Church has, with varying fortunes and in varying degrees, kept alive that witness for a great majority of the English-speaking peoples. It is true that for fully four hundred years Protestantism has intensified and deepened a certain portion of that witness and has thus prepared a most valuable contribution towards the Church of the future. And it is towards the Church of the future that M. Loisy's gaze is set. Do we, who are not of the Roman Communion, look elsewhere ? The enlightened Protestant will hardly deny that, owing mainly to the circumstances of its origin, the religious witness of Protestantism has been partial ; that it has unduly depressed the social element in religion which may be fairly claimed as the original and characteristic element of the religion of the kingdom ; that its effect, even its

conscious purpose, has been to create a religious *élite*.
And the enlightened Anglican will admit that, while
Anglicanism has been privileged by its historical fortunse
to share to some extent in the fulness of the Catholic
and in the intensity of the Protestant witness, it yet
appeals only to a portion of a single race. Even we,
who are Anglicans or Protestants, may recognize the
prerogative opportunity of the Church of Rome to be
the centre of a reformed and, if not reunited, at least
federated and mutually intelligent, Christendom.

Are we satisfied with a Christian witness which in its
best moods is fragmentary and partial, in its worst is
discordant and mutually unintelligent ?   M. Loisy is no
more satisfied than we with that spirit of absolutism,
which throughout Christendom, and not in the Roman
Church alone, has been, and is, the spirit of discord.
But he at least is working for the better day.   He has
constituted himself, by the work to which he has devoted
his life, at once the intellectual and the spiritual protagonist of a new reform.   He is the clear-sighted, patient
antagonist of that absolutism, intellectual or ecclesiastical,
which, at least in our day, whatever services it may have
rendered in the past, threatens the very foundations of
the Society of the Friends of Christ.   But he has the
historical sense.   He sees how the Divine purposes
accomplish themselves in the most unexpected ways.
He sees the absolutism against which he fights already
self-strangled by the contradictions inherent in the
logical completion of its idea as affirmed by militant
Ultramontanism.   Why should he despair of the Church,
which has hitherto, and often as it would seem by the

most contradictory processes, preserved the witness of Christianity for the greater part of the West ? Or, again, why should he be thought to despise the value of the religious witness of Protestantism because he sees how partial that witness is ? Probably no one understands more fully than he the import of those words of M. Marcel Hébert, uttered while he was still a member of the Roman Church. " Catholicism must endure its Protestantism, and in the day that it does so there will be an end of the latter." That is the only possible method of what is called the Reunion of Christendom. If the Church of the Christendom of the future is to be, if there is to be again one Society of the Friends of Christ, on such terms alone will it be formed.

CHAPTER VIII

M. LABERTHONNIÈRE'S RELIGIOUS PHILOSOPHY*

IT is now ten years since M. Blondel in his famous Sor- September 16, 1903 bonne thesis launched that view of religious certainty which has since been known as the New Apologetic, or the Apologetic of Immanence. During those ten years it has been the mark for innumerable criticisms from the outraged devotees of the traditional scholastic dogmatism, criticisms which must have inspired those who had at heart the extension of the area of faith with a profound satisfaction that the traditionalists were no longer left in exclusive possession of the field of religious defence. Meanwhile " L'Action " has long been out of print, and M. Blondel's scrupulous conscientiousness and, one is sorry to have to add, his delicate health have too long delayed that revised edition which for some years his admirers have been eagerly awaiting. It is therefore with all the greater pleasure that we hail the appearance of these admirable essays in religious philosophy written by the most original of M. Blondel's disciples, Père Laberthonnière of the Oratory. They are marked throughout by a closeness of reasoning, a controversial forbearance and urbanity (where controversy could not be avoided), a depth of religious feeling, and a rich human warmth which witness at once to a profound intellect and a saintly soul.

* " Essais de Philosophie Religieuse." Par le Père L. Laberthonnière. Paris : Lethielleux, 1903.

The New Apologetic, as it has been called, is, like many things which are hailed as new by injudicious friends or contemptuously labelled new by interested enemies, not new at all, but exactly as old as human faith. That is its own first claim. It is merely the conscious analysis of the process by which the religious life has always attained, and must always attain, to the certainty of vital truth— a process which we may call unconscious, in so far as it has not adequately realised itself in terms of thought. It is only the experience of the mystics and of all great religious souls caught in the living act and made intelligible. Its value as apologetic lies in the fact that it finds in life itself, in the total activity of living wills, the only trustworthy means of affirming reality. The traditional apologetic has failed because it is lifeless, because it has attempted to substitute an abstraction of thought for a living belief. It has thought to present the eternal mysteries of God, of the universe, of the soul as rigidly ascertained facts of completed knowledge, not as the increasingly ascertainable certainties of a knowledge which grows in exact proportion as life grows. And so life—and above all life in its highest expression, the religious life—which must grow, has either languished in the prison of this intellectual dogmatism or has burst its barriers, often in the fatal belief that it had at the same time escaped the need of faith or unmasked its illusions. Père Laberthonnière is not indeed concerned to provide a new temporary expedient of religious defence in the place of one which has grown antiquated and futile. He is engaged in a much more serious task, a task of pure philosophy—that, namely, of discovering how in any truth we reach a knowledge of ultimate certainties.

But incidentally he has done something, and not merely for his own time, not only to make religious faith possible, but to demonstrate it as a necessity of life.

The method of certainty which Père Laberthonnière exposes in these essays he calls—in contrast with the empirical dogmatism of the Sensationalists and the intellectual dogmatism of the Idealists—moral dogmatism. Though during the greater part of the nineteenth century metaphysics was under a cloud, the ultimate problem of philosophy still remains the metaphysical one of the nature of reality. And with that question must always be allied the further question of how we can attain to the knowledge of reality. These two questions can be separated only if, and in so far as, reality is considered as something outside, and apart from, ourselves. They become vitally one when we conceive of reality as something which is affirmed by the total activity of the soul. It is the merit of these studies that they face the problem of reality in this way. To measure the value of this method it will be necessary to consider for a moment the nature of rival solutions. On the one hand, there is the metaphysical scepticism of those who deny that any certainty of reality can be attained. For them the world is a world of appearances. It is impossible to say of anything that it is, only that it appears such to such and such a one. This variety of appearance is irreducible, and the only refuge from it is to refuse to believe in or affirm any reality. Akin to this is the agnostic attitude—the admission that reality exists, but that it is altogether beyond our knowledge. On the other hand, there are the intellectual dogmatists

who think to find the real in the phenomenal, the absolute
in the relative, either by an immediate act of perception
or through the intermediary of ideas to which they give
an ontological value. It was the merit of the critical
philosophy that it exposed the contradictions and the
absurdity of this virtual identification of the phenomenal
with the real.

In this view reality is what Kant called an object—
an object either of sensation or of thought. But an
object of sensation as such is only that which we feel,
in other words a state of our own feeling. An object of
thought as such is only that which we have thought, an
abstraction of our minds from certain states of feeling.
So far the critical philosophy is completely justified.
But it is just here that Père Laberthonnière parts company with the critics and imports a new constructive
element into the problem of reality. The real is not an
object at all, but a subject. It is as subject and subject
only that we can attain to a knowledge of the real in
itself. Obviously this is a knowledge which cannot be
achieved by a single effort of the mind, or indeed by
intellectual effort at all, in so far as that effort is possible
apart from the complete activity of the will. It is a
knowledge which involves moral activity, and sensation
and thought only in so far as they are part of that activity
or minister to it. For, because sensation and thought
cannot of themselves bring us into contact with the real,
it does not follow that they can only land us in delusion.
On the contrary, in so far as they contribute to moral
effort they are themselves helping to constitute the real
which everywhere underlies the phenomenal. Their

report, indeed, of objects felt and thought is not the truth of that reality which is one and permanent ; but, as we have seen, a record of states of our own feeling or of abstractions from them. They do not bring reality to us. It is just we who can import reality into them. Our sensations and our ideas contain just as much reality as there is already in ourselves, in our active, conscious energy. Life does not passively receive truth ; it actively constitutes it.

Let us examine a little more closely how this method of attaining certainty of the real works. How, for instance, do we attain to a sense of the real, of being, which is one and permanent, in ourselves, or in the world outside ourselves ? We may for the present overlook the answer of the sceptics, for that answer is a mere denial of the possibility of any such attainment. For them, neither in themselves nor in the world, is there any permanent reality which may be known. But the intellectual dogmatists assert that such reality is knowable. It is only necessary to open the eyes of the mind in order to receive it. But, as we have already seen, the critical philosophy has sufficiently demonstrated that the world thus conceived is not the world of permanent reality, but of a particular manner of seeing. That is sufficiently evident from the fact that the world has been conceived in so many different manners. Or to take another example from Père Laberthonnière himself :— " Under the word God have been ranged and continue to be ranged conceptions often very different the one from the other. The God of the Gospel is not the God of Plato or of Aristotle. The God of Descartes is not the God of Leibnitz. And the God whom certain Neapolitan brigands call to their aid in the commission of a crime has no resemblance to the God of St. Vincent de Paul or of the rest of the saints." In short, we all desire that what we think should be the truth, and the truth reduced to this kind of static abstraction is a mere record of some phase of human desire. We have, as it were, intellectually photographed a purely temporary and relative aspect of ourselves, and tried thenceforward to impose it upon the world as unalterable truth. We thought we had discovered the authentic figure of reality, and we find that, after all, it is only our own intellectual shadow, or, rather, the permanent spectre of some momentary dead-and-gone phase of ourselves.

But just here is the clue to the attainment of the only knowledge of reality which is possible for us. If we could attain to something like unity and permanence in ourselves, then we should inevitably import that measure of reality into even our ideas, we should so far help to constitute truth. Now, of course, it is clear that man, just because he is man, can never attain to absolute unity and permanence in himself, and can never, therefore, give birth to ideas which will even represent the absolute truth. But none the less man does attain to a kind of provisional sense of unity and permanence in every act of the moral will ; for the moral will is the act by which man affirms himself amid the shows of things that change and pass alike within and without, by which he constitutes himself through whatever is real and permanent in the phenomenal and impermanent. It is the act by which man loves God and seeks to lift himself into union with the Divine will. It is the act of love and not of mere desire, the act by which man would transform himself into the nature of God, according to the will of God, not the act by which he would seek to accommodate God's will to his own. It is, therefore, the act to which life can put no term, the act which must continue and deepen so long as man continues and grows. It is only through this act, the uninterrupted and growing act of life, that man can attain to the sense of permanence in himself.

And through it also he attains to the certainty of God, he affirms God. Yet he does not reach this certainty, he does not make this affirmation, apart from God. On the contrary, it is just because God is the principle of his life that either is possible. If God were apart from man, he might strain for ever in vain to reach reality, or, rather, he would never have made the attempt. It is just because God is in him that he has never ceased to make the attempt. Yet this fact of the Divine immanence is no part of a mere Pantheistic conception. Nor, on the other hand, does it need to be corrected by some crude notion of spatial transcendence. Its real corrective is suggested in the reality of man's will. God is not only the principle of man's life by which every faculty and capacity of action which he possesses exist. He is also the End after which man must continually strive in constituting himself as a reality. So it is God Who strives with him as the principle by which he is able to strive at all. Yet it is he who chooses to bring the principle into action, who makes it his own in action, who calls God into that activity by which he works towards God as his end. This is the Divine co-operation through which in the life of the moral will man attains to the certainty of being, one and permanent. It is a doctrine of will and liberty in which, nevertheless, man is utterly dependent upon God, and in which indeed, in a sense, God condescends to be dependent upon man. Père Laberthonnière puts it with a fervour of almost lyrical audacity :—

" It seems as though God Who wills us and loves us were as it were enlarged by us in His own being. In loving Him we help Him to rediscover Himself in us as we rediscover ourselves in Him. He comports Himself with us as if He had need of us in order to be. Just as we affirm ourselves freely by Him, so He by us freely affirms Himself ; yet with this difference—that we, if we willed to affirm ourselves without Him, would lose ourselves, while He could affirm Himself without us and yet lose nothing of the fulness of His being."

It is almost unnecessary to add that it is through the same activity of the moral will that Père Laberthonnière conceives the possibility of our affirming reality of beings other than ourselves. Here again it is this same activity, it is the life of love, which helps to constitute that reality. The same co-operation exists between man and man as between man and God, and exists on the same terms. All affirmations of reality are moral affirmations, and are worth just what those who make them are worth. And in proportion as the interpenetration of human life by mutual intelligence and love proceeds, men will awaken to the value not merely of one another, but of the

differences through which they express their certainty of
the real.   Truth, in so far as it can be committed to propositions, will be the result of the natural interaction and
fusion of the highest, that is, the most vital, individual
certainties.   Above all, truth so reached will never be
static, a hard, fixed, self-sufficient statement, independent
of life.   It will be, rather, dynamic, a rational point of
departure for life setting forth upon its new moral ventures.
It will be truth committing itself in absolute faith to the
hazards of such ventures.   The only object of each fresh
harvest of truth is to become seed for a new sowing in
the human will, and assuredly no one can say of what
form or quality the new harvest will be.   That will
depend upon the healthiness and productiveness of the
soil.   It is always an affair of life, and our anxiety ought
to be rather about the character of the life than about
the aspect of formal truth which the life may assimilate.

This is the merest suggestion of the matter of these
interesting essays.   But by those who would learn what
a new and living force Père Laberthonnière has brought
into the usually arid region of religious apologetics, he
must be read and not merely read about.   There is a
fascination of literary style in these essays, blended with
a kind of spiritual fragrance, which it is impossible to
convey to others.   They burn occasionally with the
passion of some mystical poem.   And yet through all
the glow and the glamour the close, sustained, un-
halting argument pursues its easy way.   This is indeed
to write on the philosophy of religion so that men may
read.   *O si sic omnes !*

CHAPTER IX

M. HOUTIN ON AMERICANISM

February, 1904 SAINTE-BEUVE once said admirably that in matters of art and literature the judgment of the foreign public was as it were the judgment of a contemporary posterity. The aphorism of the great critic implies for the competent historian of contemporary events the supreme virtue of detachment from contemporary prejudice—a virtue, like most, hard to acquire. But at least the measure of the historian's success will be best tested by the impression his work produces on those who are outside the area of conflict and immediate interest. It is the distinction of the younger school of French historians and sociologists that they leave on the outsider the impression of a scrupulous honesty and a genuine detachment in the use of their materials. M. Houtin, by his works on the Biblical question among French Catholics during the nineteenth century, and on the Apostolicity of the Churches of France, revealed himself as a distinguished and worthy representative of this school. He has sustained, indeed enhanced, his reputation by the book which he has just published on " Americanism."

This book is, as the French say, " *bien documenté.*" M. Houtin lets events narrate themselves out of the mouths of those who took part in them. And the result is an impression of those events which is living and actual

104

in a very satisfying degree. It might, indeed, at first sight seem impossible to give the effect of historical symmetry and completeness to a movement which is yet proceeding. But somehow M. Houtin achieves the impossible. And if I may venture an explanation of his success, I would say that it is because he has imaginatively projected himself beyond the furthest limits of the movement with which he is dealing. He feels that he has merely written the historical prologue to a great drama which is already beginning to unfold itself upon the stage of religious history. That will be the interest of Americanism in the near future. That is the interest which M. Houtin has subtly caught and deftly managed to convey to the sympathetic reader. And it is just that interest that redeems Americanism from a certain flaccid indecision which is a feature of all movements that are contemporary, that gives it due perspective and precision. If the critical and philosophic movements connected with the names of M. Loisy, M. Maurice Blondel, and Père Laberthonnière, had not come to foreshadow a theological revolution, Americanism would be unable as yet to justify its claim to the serious attention of the historian.

But M. Loisy and the others are with us, and Americanism is, therefore, important and immensely significant. And its significance is all the greater that it knew not what it was preparing. It is the magnificent irony of the spirit of life that it forces every genuine living movement to become something greater than it knows, something other and larger than it ever intended to be. The tide of life is ever setting towards an unknown

shore with a force which mocks at prevision and over-
whelms authority. Neither the "thus far will I go and
no further," nor the "thus far shalt thou go," is of any
avail against the mastery of its advance. It has been so
with Americanism. The apparent accident of a religious
movement growing naturally out of a new soil, alive
with the instinctive appreciation of a new atmosphere,
is producing results in far distant sections of the Roman
Church which will either give that Church the practical
hegemony of the Christianity of the future, or leave her
an abandoned hulk in the wake of human progress.

Let us see, then, what Americanism is. In its actual
form it has been, like so many other great movements,
the product of various causes, differing in their character
and apparent importance. This variety of origin is perhaps
most clearly demonstrated in the theological attitude of
the men who have been associated with its fortunes. It
has found devoted adherents in traditionalists like the
present Rector of the Catholic University of Washington,
or again in men like the Bishop of Peoria, who are as far
removed as possible alike from the spirit and the letter of
scholastic tradition. But the spirit of the movement is
one, and that spirit has been created and determined by
the peculiar national character of America. The ideal
of the old national groups in which Catholicism took its
definite European form was uniformity. Catholicism
was itself the chief factor in procuring and maintaining
that uniformity. But as we can now see in the case of
France, the instinct for uniformity has survived the
break-up of Catholicism. The France of the Republican
Block is just as anxious to crush out Catholicism as an

unassimilable element in a Republican State as Louis XIV
was to extinguish Protestantism in the interest of a
uniform Catholic State. America does not even regret
the impossibility for her of attaining such a uniformity.
Her very ideal is variety. It is the aspect of her national
life of which she is most proud, in which she consciously
realizes her peculiar strength. Hear, for instance, the
note of something like exultation in the words of Bishop
Spalding, of Peoria. " It is not to wealth or to numbers
that we owe our importance among the nations, but to
our having demonstrated that the respect for law is
compatible with civil and religious liberty ; that a free
people can grow and prosper and maintain order without
a Sovereign or a standing army ; that State and Church
can move in separate orbits and yet act for the common
good ; that men of different races and different beliefs
can live together in peace ; that in spite of the surprisingly
rapid development of wealth and population, in spite of
the numerous ills which have resulted from it, the tendency
to healthiness of thought and feeling has prevailed, thus
clearly revealing the vigor of our life and institutions ;
that government by the majority, when men have faith
in God and in the advance of knowledge, is after all the
wisest and justest form of government." These are words
which, perhaps, only an American could have spoken,
which at least only an American has any right to speak.

Americanism has its origin in the recognition by
American Catholicism of the psychological climate (if I
may steal or borrow Mr. Balfour's phrase) to which it
had to accommodate itself, and in the instinctive effort
to accommodate itself to it. How much of change this

effort was to entail was not of course at once perceived. Its extent is not perhaps yet quite realized by the American Church itself. It is this perfectly natural fact, rather than any conscious insincerity, which accounts for the momentary confusion into which the famous letter of Leo XIII to Cardinal Gibbons seemed to throw some of the leading representatives of Americanism. They simply did not know how far they had gone. None the less the results are there, unmistakable for the careful and detached observer. All that Catholicism is in its age-long growth out of a European soil—I do not of course include England—it is ceasing to be in America, and is becoming something other than and strongly contrasted with it. While in Europe Catholicism distrusts and even hates democracy, and still applauds, both in theory and practice, the doctrines of the Syllabus, in America it shares to the full the grateful and exuberant confidence in the democratic system and temper of government which is the most distinctive element of the national policy. Naturally such a difference as this affects the whole attitude of the Church towards national and civic affairs. In so far as all its outward activity is concerned, it is no longer, as in Europe, the implacably hostile rival of the State, but one corporate force among many co-operating heartily and on equal terms in the common action of the State. Even on the thorny question of education the Church has not failed in her devotion to the ideal of the Republic, and compromises like that known as the Poughkeepsie experiment* testify to a

* At Poughkeepsie, in the State of New York, the School Board for some years rented the Catholic schools, which thus became State

praiseworthy largeness of view alike on her part and on the part of local Education Authorities.

But it is not merely in the outward activity of the Church as a corporate body that a change has declared itself. It is just as much in her more intimate work as a director of souls. The uniform ideal of character, or rather of temperament, which obtains throughout the old Catholic world, and has actually produced a common type of character, at least a type marked by an apparent uniformity, has yielded in America to the urgency of the national ideal of individuality. Where enterprise and initiative count for so much in all fields of action, it is not likely that they could for long be excluded from the field of religious feeling and its expression. And the change which was being unconsciously wrought by the necessary action of changed conditions found conscious expression in the thought and aim of one man—Isaac Thomas Hecker. Hecker, who was born in New York, in 1819, of German parents, was one of those spirits, of whom the Nineteenth Century knew so many, who suffered from the intellectual anarchy and confusion of an over-confident and aggressive individualism. He found, again like so many others of his time, in the authoritative claim of the Roman Church exactly the rest, or rather the support, he needed. But he took with him into the Roman fold his Protestant feeling for individual initiative and variety of expression in matters

schools during school hours, but reverted to the absolute use of the Catholic body outside those hours. The Catholic teachers were recognised by the Board, and religious instruction could be given by them at any time outside the ordinary school hours of nine to three. The same experiment was tried on a larger scale in the State of Georgia.

religious. The watchword of his school was the necessity to a complete Christian life of the active virtues as contrasted with the passive virtues of absolute submission and obedience to authority which the old Catholicism had so sedulously cultivated. He depreciated the contemplative life as unsuited to the religious needs of the modern world, and especially of American life. He extolled and aimed at developing the social activity of the Church. He claimed free play for, and full recognition of, the action of the Divine Spirit in the individual life. Authority was but the background against which the multiform energies of the Spirit in individuals were thrown into relief, perhaps better the bond by which in their free movement they were held together. It was from Hecker that men like Cardinal Gibbons, Archbishop Ireland, and Bishop Spalding drew their inspiration. Impartial and capable observers have again and again described the results. One of the latest of them, M. Bargy, has summarised his observations in the statement that there is a new fact in the religious world, that there is a type of religion which is peculiarly American. To this type, he says, all the American Churches are conforming more and more, to such an extent that they resemble one another more than any one of them its Mother Church in the Old World. The note of this American type of religion is the light stress laid upon all forms of dogmatic statement and teaching, and an immense and ever-growing social activity. " It is a religion of humanity grafted on Christianity," says M. Bargy. And again, " The American religion has always as its aim the well-being of the race. It is the poetry of citizenship." And

M. Houtin, echoing M. Bargy, sums up the whole matter
thus :—" If we wish to characterize the very essence of
the religious evolution in the United States, we must say
that it is drawing all the sects alike in the direction
of what we call in Europe Liberal Protestantism." It
is not perhaps exactly how even the most advanced
Americanist would wish it to be expressed. But if a
movement is to be judged by the tendencies of its greatest
minds, then those who are acquainted with the writings
of Bishop Spalding will recognize, if not the perfect
adequacy, at least the general truth, of M. Houtin's
estimate of the share of Americanism in the common
trend of American religion. It may be that M. Houtin
is nearer the truth as to the general temper of the Roman
Church in America when he likens its spirit, as he has
done in another place, to that of the Anglican Church.
It is a resemblance of whose suggestion no member of
that Church need be ashamed. But perhaps the closest
resemblance to Americanism, as I have realized it in
M. Houtin's interesting pages, is to be found in the ideal
of Catholicism which haunts the mind of my friend, Mr.
Headlam, and is witnessed to by his Guild of St. Matthew.

CHAPTER X

1904

THE year 1904 has given us at least two contributions of the first importance to the elucidation of the Liberal theological movement in the Roman Church. During the first three months of the year a defence and reinforcement of M. Loisy's position, in the form of letters addressed by a priest to his friend, appeared in the *Annales de Philosophie Chrétienne*. The authorship of these anonymous letters has been generally attributed to a well-known Italian theologian. The second document of importance was Baron von Hügel's reply in the *Quinzaine* for June 1st to certain articles of M. Maurice Blondel in the same review, in which that philosopher denied the right of historical criticism to complete autonomy in the field of Gospel history.

I

M. Blondel attempted to defeat the critics by an ingenious turning movement. He did not venture to defend the position occupied by so many conservative, and especially English conservative scholars, that the application of critical methods of enquiry to the Gospel history has left the traditional view of that history practically intact. He admitted that theological criticism, released from the control of theological pre-conceptions, was justified of the destructive conclusions

112

which it had reached. But just because those conclusions seemed to him to be destructive of the integrity of Christian doctrine, he denied altogether the right of criticism to autonomy in the religious domain. It was impossible to admit the legitimacy of a method which thus rendered insecure the very foundations of Christianity, the supreme expression of the religious faith and hope of mankind. M. Blondel's way of meeting the difficulty was characteristic. It was from his own philosophy of "action," from his conception of the totality of life as the medium through which all religious revelation is given, and more especially the medium through which alone it can be apprehended, that he drew the materials for his defence of the traditional position. Naturally, for a scholastic his argument would have no force whatever. The scholastic, to whom the defence of the Christian faith is an exercise in pure dialectic, is forced to assert the integrity of the Christian revelation in its original form, or rather to maintain the formal identity of the present sum of Christian dogma with the revealed doctrine of the Gospels. To that end he has simply neutralised the whole territory of formal Revelation. He has shut it off from the operation of the methods of critical experiment and conflict by which truth is ordinarily established. Revelation is intangible and subject to no possibility or degree of doubt. If, as a concession to the prevailing insanity of the time, he admits the application of critical method at all, he admits it only on the condition that it establishes his case. He is as little likely to sympathise with M. Blondel's subtle method of evading the force of critical conclusions as he is to admit either the legitimacy of those conclusions or the right of the critics to reach them.

M. Blondel, then, admits that modern critical history is a science which, like every other science, has its own characteristic method. He admits that this science must, both by its own nature and in virtue of the historical character of the Gospel, deal with the historical facts which the Gospels record. But he denies its sufficiency to establish even the historical truth of the record ; and he denies it, as I have said, in virtue of that philosophy of " action " which is his own profound contribution to the religious apologetic of our time. For M. Blondel, reality, the ultimately real in every life, is immediately revealed in the confused activity of spirit, an activity which necessarily eludes exact apprehension or definition. The real, therefore, is not and never can be completely given in intellectual concepts which are of their very nature secondary and derived. It is given in that from which these inadequate and often mutilating concepts are derived. It is by a kind of sublime spiritual intuition, determined by our common share in ultimate reality, that each life enters into a knowledge of every other. That power of entry into the secret reality of other life depends upon the degree in which the soul that would know has developed in itself a complete and harmonious quality of spiritual activity. Now it is evident that in the life of our Lord that reality was given in the most exhaustive and perfect form which it can attain under the conditions of humanity. And it is equally evident that the knowledge of that life depends upon the increasing power which humanity is gaining through its developed spiritual activity of apprehending the inexhaustible mystery of reality revealed in it. M. Blondel therefore argues that even the history of the human life of Jesus must be read in the light of the knowledge which Christian humanity has gained through its vital experience of all that was contained and involved in the personality of Jesus. In His personality, as it was manifested in Galilee 2000 years ago, all that progressive and ever-enlarging Christian experience has since discovered in it was already revealed. But historical criticism cannot and does not even pretend to do more than establish the impression which the personality of our Lord left upon the minds of His contemporaries. It is evident, therefore, that it is unequal to the task of giving a true record even of our Lord's human life. That life contained mysteries which its contemporary observers did not so much as suspect ; and those mysteries may well have expressed themselves in outward events and happenings, the true nature and purport of which escaped those who actually saw them, but were gradually revealed to those who may not have seen them with the eyes of the flesh, but meditated upon them through the vision of the spirit. Thus the Synoptics may have preserved for us a more faithful record of what contemporaries saw in the life of Jesus, while the Fourth Gospel may still give us the truer account not only of the inner life of Jesus, but even of its phenomenal happenings.

This is by no means the whole of M. Blondel's argument. But it seems to be the most important point which he makes as against the claim of criticism to disengage the measure of exact historical truth contained in the Gospel records. And it is to this point chiefly that Baron von

Hügel addresses his reply. That reply delivers us at once from the tangle in which the subtlety of M. Blondel's argument had involved us. It seems almost the object, it certainly would be the effect, of arguments like those of M. Blondel, to lead us back, by way of a life-philosophy, into all the dangerous delusions with which the monopoly claimed by a mere intellectual dialectic in the exposition of Christian truth had for so long beset the path of the Christian apologist. However little M. Blondel may himself intend it, the effect of his position would be to consecrate afresh, and in a far more subtle and dangerous manner, the formal adequacy of dogma. That this is far from M. Blondel's own intention, all those who know his writings will at once conclude. He has indeed done as much as any man of his time to demonstrate the merely representative character of dogma, to establish alike the distinction and the connection between the reality lived and felt and the reality thought. Yet there is here an evident tendency to obliterate the distinction and to resolve the connection into an actual identity. For the establishment of the distinction depends upon a work of analysis which can only be accomplished in the workshop of history. If history may not give its evidence as to the growth of dogma freely, if its witness on that head is denied or tampered with, then the block of formal dogma remains. M. Blondel may still distinguish for himself between the witness of dogma to the reality revealed immediately in life, and its witness to the same reality mediated through changing habits of thought. But there is no longer any objective measure or criterion of such distinction. The formal block of dogma is reinstated by M. Blondel's efforts. And the scholastics will turn the result to their own account without even thanking him for his part in procuring it.

What Baron von Hügel so admirably enforces in his reply to M. Blondel is the necessity of seizing the objective element in dogmatic statements as a guide and standard in their analysis. Now that element is primarily the actual phenomenal facts and happenings which first stimulated the life of faith to see in them the further objective reality of spirit, the affirmation of which is the very essence of dogmatic truth. This truth may of course be mediated to us through much historical illusion, and has as matter of fact been often so mediated. But we feel that such mediation of the truth is necessarily imperfect or provisional. We ought at least to know the spiritual truth the more adequately, the more perfectly we can establish the phenomenal events through which it was given. This is the value of criticism, that it alone can disengage the actual historical facts which were both the occasion of faith and the medium which conveyed and suggested the special content of its intuitions. It may therefore legitimately claim for its conclusions in its own kind and on its own level of enquiry freedom from revision or amplification on the part of any external interest or authority. In other words, criticism in its own field must be autonomous. The facts were what they were, and cannot be altered by doctrinal considerations of a later date. In reaching a conclusion as to what the facts actually were, no dogmatic afterthought or after-vision of faith has the right to intervene.

It may be that scholarship has not yet reached an

agreement on the exact measure of the facts which underlie the Gospel record, though Baron von Hügel seems to agree with M. Loisy that the extent and degree of the doubt which still subsists among competent scholars is so small as not materially to affect the essential features of the Gospel history as passed through the critical sieve. But in any case critical scholarship must continue its task until agreement is secured. That is beginning to be the insistent claim of religion itself. It does not want fancy facts, facts fashioned or coloured by some religious preconception of a moment as to what the facts ought to be. Starting from its initial faith in God, it is confident that the actual facts of God's world are sufficient for the revelation of God, that in them as they have actually happened God has always declared Himself. And especially it is beginning to feel that there is nothing but gain for its cause and for its influence over men in the new verdict of criticism about the facts of our Lord's life, which is bringing those facts into closer accord with the deepest elements in men's ordinary experience.

Such relative autonomy, therefore, as history legitimately claims in any portion of its own domain it can and must claim in the peculiarly religious portion also. There, too, it is required to do its own special work by its own special methods. It must make by the use of those methods as accurate report as it can of the facts through which the Christian revelation was given to men. It cannot, indeed, in any wise impose either positively or negatively a religious meaning upon those facts. The religious significance of the facts for those who saw them face to face was the work of faith. Their religious significance for those who have heard of them ever since has also been the work of faith. The facts in their phenomenal or formal aspect, the only aspect perceptible to the senses of the contemporaries of Jesus, had no power of imposing a religious revelation upon those His contemporaries. Nor have the facts as mere happenings, when transmitted to us, any such power. It is that intuitive vision of reality which springs out of the deepest and most harmonious activity of all our faculties realised in the moral will and conscience, that vision which we call faith, that alone reveals to us the religious value and witness of the facts. Yet it is not possible to maintain, as M. Blondel does, that the religious significance of the facts once perceived may legitimately react upon them so as to change even their phenomenal character, or rather (it may be more just to M. Blondel's thought to say) so as to reveal in them a character which they actually had as events in space and time, and yet which no one who had experience of them as events in space and time seems to have recognised or reported. What the facts phenomenally were, what, that is to say, they were for the eyes and ears of those who observed and reported them, that they remain for the historian. What they were in themselves, what they witnessed to of the character and action of eternal reality, that the historian as historian has no competence to declare. It is true that since the historian and the man of faith are often, and ought normally to be, merely different functions or aspects of the same individual, some confusion of the two characters is inevitable in every judgment. Yet that does not justify such confusion. The concrete living reality can only be made an object of knowledge by our recognizing the distinction between its phenomenal and spiritual aspects, and respecting as fully as possible the conditions under which each is apprehended. Baron von Hügel has happily disengaged what is vitally true in M. Blondel's contention from what is misleading and dangerous in the following sentences :—

" It is undoubtedly true that every saintly soul which has been inspired by the Christian life and by the love of our Lord has helped in its measure to penetrate, to explicitate, to translate, and to make fruitful the glorious reality of the truth and grace of Jesus Christ. And so in a very real sense, we can speak of the earthly life of the heavenly Christ Himself, that is to say, of the effects wrought by the Eternal Christ upon this earth. These spiritual facts, too, have a historical side and are presented under phenomenal forms which the Church observes, collects, and registers, and in which she sees, again under the influence of the heavenly life of the Christ, the growing apprehension and indefinite application of the events of His past life on earth. Yet this series of phenomena does not complete our critical knowledge of the earthly life of Jesus. Of this terrestrial and phenomenal life we shall gain no new knowledge, so long, at least, as no new document is discovered, or no more scholarly analysis of the documents which we know already is offered us."

II

But it is sufficiently obvious that M. Blondel's retreat to positions which only Scholasticism can effectively occupy is due to à priori considerations. It is his fear

of an inductive Christology that has compelled him to
wrest his own theory of the method and character of our
knowledge of reality to the defence of conclusions which
it does not naturally support, which indeed it expressly
controverts. It is natural that the scholastic theology,
with its strong deductive bias, should virtually annul
the humanity of our Lord in its theory of the union of the
human nature of Jesus with God. Starting from its
abstract theory of the nature of Divinity and of the
necessary conditions of its self-manifestation, it imposes
these conditions upon the facts. The omniscience and
omnipotence of God, for instance, must be present in
their full expression in every manifestation of Himself.
These purely abstract conceptions, which rebuke all our
concrete experience and escape all our concrete knowledge,
are used to determine, before all examination of the facts,
the nature of our Lord's complex personality and even
the events of His earthly life. Miracles in the crudest
evidential sense, as the witnesses of unlimited and even
unintelligible power, were not only the natural accompani-
ment, but the very essence, of our Lord's activity. It
was necessary, in virtue of His nature, that God should
so act; and therefore God in union with the human life
of Jesus did so act. Again, because of the omniscience
of God, Jesus through His union with God must have
had God's complete and inclusive knowledge of all
events, past, present, and to come, and must have had
it, without limit or possibility of growth, from the cradle
of Bethlehem to the Cross of Calvary.

Now for M. Blondel, who holds that the supernatural
action of God in man consists in a stimulation of his

natural active powers to an ever-growing apprehension of the Divine, it might have seemed that such a conception would prove unsatisfying. Yet he falls back upon something very much akin to it, in fear apparently of losing all real hold upon our Lord's Divinity. Here his timidity is rebuked, not only by Baron von Hügel, but by the author of the "Lettres Romaines." Both these writers remind us of the very obvious fact that all apprehension proceeds from the known to the unknown, or rather, from the better-known to the less-known. Our knowledge of God is indeed the effect of a Divine grace ; but that grace acts through our natural powers and through our use of them in penetrating to the secret of certain actual concrete facts. It is through these familiar facts that God reveals Himself to us. Without our more immediate knowledge of man we could never have reached to the more distant knowledge of God. All our conceptions of God are necessarily anthropomorphic. The more we come to know of the nature and conditions of human personality, the more likely are we to frame analogies of the Divine nature which will be at least less discordant with its reality. The essential difference between scholastic and modern theology is not so much a difference between the use of the deductive and inductive methods, but proceeds rather from their different conceptions of human personality. Scholasticism is no more free than any other system from the necessity of finding its theological starting-point in the known. It, too, is to some degree inductive in its method. But it gives an absolute value to a conception of God which was founded in a less perfect notion of what is greatest and most worthy in human character, and deduces from that imperfect conception even the character of the facts of God's self-revelation. With a less imperfect, but still perfectible and altogether relative view of what constitutes worth in personality, and of the conditions under which that worth is achieved, we not only do not need to impose upon history a particular view of the facts which will accord with the supposed necessities of a Divine revelation, but are compelled to ascertain as accurately as we can the facts through which the Divine revelation was conveyed, in order to a better apprehension of it through the supernatural grace of faith.

These are the positions enforced with a convincing power by both Baron von Hügel and the author of the "Lettres Romaines." If, says the former, we knew beforehand the full nature of the mystery of Divinity in Jesus, if our conceptions of Divinity were adequate, then we could understand the application of *à priori* methods, even to the establishment of the facts of His life. If, on the other hand, as the Christian faith asserts, the reality of the Divine union with the humanity of Jesus is unique, and for our intelligence of an inexhaustible import, then it becomes us to learn in all humility by the patient processes of critical science what the facts of His human life really were. To force the facts to our conception of what they ought to be is an instance of spiritual pride and unteachableness, not the less reprehensible because it may be the result of ignorance or of intellectual sloth. "This method," says the author of the "Lettres Romaines," "is in itself illogical. It is not by *à priori* methods that we can determine the character of what comes from God or is united to God, but only by *à posteriori* methods. What would be thought of a philosopher who should reason thus :—' The world was created by God, therefore there can be no evil in it.' We should reply, ' Examine the physical reality of things, before dictating to God the law of His creation. Formerly theologians asserted that Holy Scripture was inspired by God, which was true. But they concluded from that premiss that it must therefore contain truth as to the order of nature, which is a false consequence deduced *à priori*. And is not this reasoning on a level with that of the theologians who say, ' Jesus was God-man or Man-God : therefore His humanity united to His divinity cannot have been subject either to ignorance or to development ? ' ' Can ' or ' cannot '—all that is mere creation on our part. It is not our business to create things, but to ascertain them. *À priori* a God-man of imperfect knowledge (in his capacity as man, that is to say) is no greater challenge to our ways of thought and feeling than a God-man simply, or than a suffering God-man. I am much mistaken or we have conceived God uniting Himself to man as something which has changed man, or again of man united to God as something which is no longer man. The Christ of the theologians floats indefinitely between real humanity and divinity. But no, we must remind ourselves that Jesus was a real man, like to His brethren *in everything* save sin only. We must seek in accordance with the documents the measure of the veritable results which were effected in His humanity by its union with the Divinity. If the documents tell us that Jesus developed in His human nature, that His knowledge was imperfect, that He was tempted, that He suffered, we must believe them. And if anyone is offended, we can only repeat the words of Christ Himself :—' *Beatus qui non fuerit scandalizatus in me.*' We can only remind him that the Jews also were offended by the idea of a crucified Man-God, and that yet St. Paul neither denied nor minimised that ignominy, the *opprobrium crucis*. In the same way we to-day must not minimise the real and complete humanity of Jesus, body, soul, intelligence, and will. We must boldly assert it. According both to history and to dogma, the Christ was a real, complete, and perfect man—perfect, we mean, in His human quality."

Nor do the writers from whom I have quoted at all shirk the consequences of our Lord's imperfect human knowledge, of His ignorance of the future course of events in detail, including the outward character and destiny of His own Church. Far from shirking them, they find in that ignorance the strongest proof of our Lord's human greatness, and that in accordance with the surest conclusions of modern psychology as to the nature and true greatness of human personality. " It seems," says Baron von Hügel, " that for M. Blondel the Divine-human action of Christ, in order that it might be really worthy of a God made man, really capable of saving us, required that the human consciousness and reflection of Jesus should embrace that action and be entirely equal to it at the very moment when it was determined and effected. That surely is contradicted by all analogies drawn from the lives of the saints, and especially of those who most nearly approached the character of Jesus. Who indeed demands, whether that he may admire the greatness of these saints or that he may profit by their help, that there should be even a distant approximation between their actions and a clear consciousness of all that was implied in them ? Is it not exactly the contrary which always happens ? We may admit that St. Paul and the *Poverello* enjoyed an infinitely deeper spiritual insight than our own, and that they heroically followed that inner light. Yet do we not regard them as all the greater and more helpful by their example exactly because in every one of their acts they passed beyond what their consciousness explicitly realized at the moment they wrought them ? That is assuredly the most profound and touching characteristic of all specifically human life ; and how could our Lord, Who came precisely that He might draw men, have failed of this same characteristic, or not have been at this point also truly man ? "

The author of the " Lettres Romaines " discusses the same question of the limitations of our Lord's human knowledge, of His defective and even erroneous prevision of the future, in special connection with the foundation and growth of the Christian Church. And he, too, enforces the same conclusion as to the true human greatness which this outstripping of conscious knowledge by inspired action witnesses to and reveals. " Psychology," he says, " in union with history, teaches us that the men who have been truly great have never foreseen the historical details of their enterprise, that the latter has always surpassed their designs, their conscious purpose, even their personal prevision. St. Francis of Assisi had

no thought of a new religious order. Yet that is what
issued from the movement which he impressed upon the
souls of his friends and contemporaries. Now if that in
no wise lessens the greatness of St. Francis, is the greatness of Jesus any the more lessened by the admission
that He did not foresee the long course of His Church's
progress ? It was from Him and from Him alone that
it received the impulse by which it still lives after twenty
centuries of labour, of struggle, of suffering, and of joyous
fruitful life. That we may lay hold of this principle, let
us remember what recent psychology has placed in the
clearest light. The character of true greatness lies not
in consciousness, but in unconsciousness, or something
like it. When I write miserable little verses, I do so
with far more consciousness of what I want to say than
Pindar, Virgil, Shelley, or Victor Hugo felt when they
sang the most profound and inspired of their songs. It
seems almost as if the truth of this position had been
reached expressly to remove the scandal caused to some
minds by the idea of a Christ who was, not altogether
unconscious indeed, but much less conscious than was
formerly supposed, in His work of founding the Church."

And the same author sums up his argument in these
words :—" Once more, the Christ of criticism, that is to
say the real Christ, is not inferior to the Christ of learned
or pious fancies. He is greater. He has the specific
character of true greatness. For that greatness does
not consist in the conscious prevision of the work which
one accomplishes. Rather it is measured by the
superiority of the work over the fully conscious intention.
It is to be found in a certain unconsciousness. Psychology

discovers this unconsciousness in all those who have had the right to say :—' *Est deus in nobis, agitante calescimus illo.*' And who has ever had that right in equal measure with the Lord Jesus ? "

These two documents, so contrasted in their style and in the individual character which shines through them, concur in their critical view of the facts of the Christian revelation, and in their exposition of the certainties which faith discovers in those facts. They will do much to clear up some of the issues which have been raised by the Loisy writings. The truth of history consists in the establishment of what has actually happened and appeared in space and time. It is necessary in order to reach such truth to weigh all the available evidence, interpreted through the medium of a matured psychology, in scales as nicely adjusted as detachment from all extraneous and disturbing preoccupations can make them. The Christian revelation was in its phenomenal vehicles and occasions a part of history, and its historical reality cannot escape the ordinary tests. But again, the Christian revelation was a Divine secret apprehended by human souls through those facts. Here, too, truth has its criteria, though they are no longer the criteria of historical truth. The criterion of spiritual truth for the Scholastic has been, as the author of the " Lettres Romaines " reminds us, a barren fixity. Its real criterion is, on the contrary, its power to produce life and to incorporate the gains of life, its intrinsic growth and its extrinsic fruitfulness.

CHAPTER XI

" IL SANTO "

WE are at a moment of critical change in the history of *April,* 1906 religion. It may be at once admitted that it is too early to estimate the full measure of the change. But certain aspects of it at least, and these the controlling ones, are already clear enough. The study of religion is passing from the region of the abstract into the region of the concrete, from the religious formula to the religious life. We are no longer satisfied with making an inventory and an assay of the contents of the theological granary. We want to see the seed growing, and to learn all we can of the abiding conditions of its growth. We are back again at the Parable of the Sower with its stress on the comparative and contrasted values of soil, and its implication that the seed sown in them all is the same seed—the universal Word of God. For us the life of the saint has supplanted in importance the doctrine of the theologian. The theological controversies of the past are almost meaningless. The theological controversies of the future are not yet defined. They must wait upon the slow results of a comprehensive and patient analysis of religious experience. The signs of this change are on all hands. A whole literature is growing up to bear witness to it and elicit or illustrate its meaning. Religious psychology vies with the history of dogma for the favour of the younger theologians, and helps

to interpret and supplement its results. The theology
which would make religion intelligible instead of burying
it under a mere heap of gratuitous unintelligibility has
had no more valuable contributions in our day than such
studies in concrete religious psychology, studies such,
for instance, as those of the Abbé Bremond on More and
Newman. And now, as was inevitable in the existing
conditions of successful literary appeal, the novel claims
its share in the work of religious renewal. Within the
past year, at least four religious novels marked by an
almost poignant sincerity have appeared. M. Rod's
" L'Indocile " is a concrete study in the conflict of actual
religious ideals. The great Styrian novelist, Rosegger,
has portrayed in a novel which has just been translated
into English, the effect of the Gospel story upon a soul
awaiting death in the silence of the condemned cell.
Madame Handel-Mazzetti's " Jesse und Maria " is a
study of the reaction upon each other of the Catholic and
Protestant types of devotion and heroism, a study which
in its justice and its sympathetic intelligence is now for
the first time possible since the sixteenth century disruption of Christendom. And the honour of this superb
act of truth, which is also a supreme act of faith, falls,
we ought to add, to a Roman Catholic writer. And,
lastly, there is Antonio Fogazzaro's " Il Santo."

It is of this last that I wish to speak here. The question
which besets the thought and possesses the heart of the
Italian novelist is the means of the Church's salvation
from the four evil spirits which assail her life—the spirit
of falsehood, the spirit of sacerdotalism (*dominazione
del clero*), the spirit of avarice, and the spirit of immobility.

For Fogazzaro, no answer to this question can be satis-
factory which would involve the destruction of the
Church's existing constitution and order. Throughout
the book there breathes a note of reverent submission to
her authority, of pious devotion to even her formal
tradition. But there breathes, too, the note of insistent
and pitiless sincerity which will recall authority to a sense
of its real spiritual mission, which will remind the formal
tradition of dogma that it is only the imperfect depositary
of the living tradition of holiness which is the Church's
past, only the provisional, if necessary, instrument of its
transmission to the future. The actual Church is not the
Kingdom of Heaven, but only its herald and servant.
But the Church that ought to be must grow out of the
Church that is, and therefore it must be free to grow out
of it. That is the responsibility which is laid upon the
momentary wielders of the Church's authority. They
are not responsible so much to the past that is half-dead,
as to the future which labours to be wholly alive. In
the loins of the present, the past and the future meet.
All of the past that can endure is that which endures
there in the act of spiritual procreation on which
the future depends. It is courageous insight into the
spiritual needs and realities of the present that justifies
authority, and not the timorous obstinacy which barri-
cades itself behind the letter of what was once a living
experience in the past. But I shall perhaps best do
justice to Fogazzaro's conception of the Church by
quoting some words which he has put into the mouth of
his saint : " The Church is the whole man, not a mere
group of outstanding and dominant ideas ; the Church

is the hierarchy with its traditional concepts, and it is
the lay world with its continuous hold upon reality, with
its continuous reaction upon tradition ; the Church is
official theology and the inexhaustible treasure of Divine
truth which reacts upon official theology ; the Church
does not die, the Church does not grow old, the Church
has in its heart more than on its lips the Living Christ,
the Church is a laboratory of truth in continuous action,
and God calls you to remain in the Church, to work in
the Church, to be in the Church fountains of living
waters." The words are addressed to those who in their
devotion to Christ had fled from the Church to the Saint
for guidance, who complained that " the Catholic Church,
which proclaims herself a minister of life, fetters and
suffocates to-day everything within her that lives with a
young and vigorous life, props up all that is falling to ruin
and decay." They no doubt express the faith in the
Church which the novelist would desire to claim as his
own. " You have turned to me," says the Saint, " without knowing what you did, to learn that the Church is
not the hierarchy only, but is the universal assembly of
the faithful, a *gens sancta ;* that from the depth of every
Christian heart may burst forth the living water of the
same fountain head, of the same Truth."

And with this conception of the Church, Fogazzaro is
able to give his answer. What is needed for the reform
of the Church is a great Saint, one of those master souls
of the great lay world, who have so often, in times past,
arisen to testify of God and His immediate present
claims. And Fogazzaro has not feared to snatch his
Saint from the gutter of modern decadence. He is no

other than that Piero Maironi, whose neurotic *liaison*
with Jeanne Dessalle was chronicled in his last novel, the
" Piccolo Mondo Moderno." Yet, daring as the venture
was, no one, I think, who reads this novel will say that it
has not succeeded. Maironi concentrates about himself
all those men of goodwill, whether formally in communion with the Church or not, whether or not they will
ever formally enter within her pale, who are naturally
Christian, who are of the soul of the Church. And we
feel that, in spite of all the occasional extravagance
of his portraiture, he had the right to draw them, and
that in him the Church was coming to her true self and
recognizing and fostering her own children.

Here is his story, very baldly told. Brought to penitence through the death of his wife and the ministrations
of a holy priest, Don Giuseppe Flores, Maironi had. fled
from his sin and from all knowledge of his old world. At
the beginning of this book he is found a poor labouring
gardener in the house of Santa Scolastica, at Subiaco.
He has left all his wealth behind him ; he lives in perpetual
fasts, submitting himself to a kind of mediæval penance ;
he spends whole nights on the mountain side in prayer ;
he has refused himself in the austerity of his penance
even the hope of assuming the dress of a lay brother of
the order. Yet he is beloved by all, and especially by
his confessor, Don Clemente, a Benedictine of saintly life,
who sees in him the Saint that is destined, perhaps, to
the mission of recalling the Church to the true following
of Christ. Don Clemente is a disciple of Giovanni Selva,
a lay philosopher whose liberal theological teaching has
already made him suspect with the authorities at Rome.

Following upon a conclave of Liberals at Selva's house, Don Clemente is denied by the new Abbot all further communication with Selva, and Maironi is banished to the Benedictine house at Jenne. Here he gains the reputation of a miracle-worker among the common people whom he tends in their sickness, till he is once more driven forth, degraded this time by deprivation of the lay brother's habit which he had been temporarily permitted to wear. Fever-stricken by fasting and exposure, he is conveyed by the Selvas to their home, and there nursed back by them to health. With returning health there comes to him the direction of the inner voice, —which, like the mystic that he is, he always trusts unhesitatingly as the immediate word of God—to repair to Rome. There he soon becomes the centre of a little band of disciples, most of them loosely connected with the Church, but many of them also just those men of goodwill for whom the Church has had no certain word of truth. To these disciples he preaches the doctrine that religion is life; that it can only be lived aright in submission to and co-operation with the Lord of Life, who is the Spirit of Truth and of charity; that every truth, however acquired, must be reverently greeted as His gift, and must be turned to account in action in His Spirit. Long ago in the days of his early penitence he had seen a vision in which he spoke out face to face with the Pope the truth that God had committed to him. There is no surprise for him, therefore, in the summons when at last it comes. The Pope himself is represented as a kind of Saint, but a Saint suffering from the impotence to which his official position and his official surroundings have

condemned him.   Maironi calls upon him to deliver the
Church from the four evil spirits which are corrupting
her life.   In acquiescent silence, the Pope hears the
terrible indictment and the confident appeal, unhesitating
as a command of God.   Maironi receives the benediction of
the Holy Father and departs into the night.   But the hour
of his final martyrdom has struck.   An attempt which the
Pope makes, in obedience to a prayer of Maironi's, to save
Selva's book from the censure of the Index is the signal
for the serpent-spring of the Vatican coterie.   The Italian
Ministry of the Interior, manageable in such emergencies
in spite of the public outlawry which it has tamely to
endure at the hands of the Vatican, is compelled to forge
some means of banishing the Saint of Jenne from Rome and
Italy, so much the better if it be under some pretext that
will cast the lasting shadow of suspicion upon his name
and character.   But neither the blustering violence nor
the wily blandishments of the modern Pilate avail to
shake the firm-set will of Maironi.   He is saved from
forced and secret deportation by the fatal fever which
finds an easy prey in his wrecked constitution and wasted
body.   One of his disciples, Mayda, the man of science,
professor in the University, at once intellectually agnostic
and profoundly religious, receives him into his house on
the Aventine.   Through the long hours of weary nights
he tenderly nurses the Saint, while by day he teaches in
his lecture room to the youth of Rome the hard stern
truth of this universe of ordered process.   Who will
apportion the rival merits of this service or of that in the
eyes of God ?   But they are not rival merits, they are
indissolubly wed.   Only, what God has joined together

we have too often put asunder. To me Mayda is one of the most attractive figures in this sincere and fearless drama of human reality. But to return to Maironi—as he feels the end draw near, he begs to be taken to the gardener's hut, there to die among the flowers which he has loved. And there he takes the last farewell of all his friends ; of the common people of the Quarter who file silently through the dying chamber to catch as a last benediction the wonder on the face of the Saint they have venerated, and alas ! after their fickle manner, rejected, too, in the hour of his disgrace ; of his little band of disciples ; of Selva, who had been for him a master of living truth ; of Don Clemente, who had been the brother of his love ; and last of all of the partner of his ancient sin, who from the crucifix which he yields to her from his dying hands receives at last the faith which her intellect had always resisted even in the days of her profound and humble penitence. So the latest of the Saints enters into the white light of the Eternal Truth, into the consuming fire of the Eternal Love, where lie the secrets of the Eternal Judgment.

Of Maironi's last words to his disciples, I would cull some fragments as only comment upon the story which I have so imperfectly told.

" Purify the faith for the full-grown for whom the food of babes is unmeet. This portion of your work is for those who are outside the Church, whether they belong to it in name or not, for those with whom your intercourse will be continual. Labour to glorify the idea of God by reverencing the truth above all things, and teaching that there is no truth which is contrary to God

and His laws. Give equal care that babes be not offered
the food which suits grown men. Let not a corrupt or
imperfect faith offend you where the life is pure and the
conscience just ; for to the infinite depths of God there
is little difference between the faith of the little child and
your own, and if the conscience of the little child be
just, if its life be pure, ye will not enter before it into the
Kingdom of Heaven. Labour for the leavening of life
by the purified faith. This work is on behalf of those
who are in the Church and will remain in it ; for those
who sincerely believe in dogmas and would willingly
believe still more of them, who sincerely believe in
miracles and would willingly believe in many more, but
who do not sincerely believe in the Beatitudes, who say
to Christ, ' Lord, Lord,' but think it too hard a matter
to do all His will, nor are zealous to search it out in the
Holy Book, and know not that religion is before all else
action and life. Those who pray much, often in an
idolatrous spirit, teach to use, over and above set prayers,
that mystical prayer also, in which is the purest faith,
the most perfect hope, the most perfect charity, which of
itself purifies the soul and the life. Do I bid you assume
publicly the work of pastors ? No ; let each one labour
in his own family, among his own friends. He who can,
let him labour with his pen. So also will ye prepare the
soil whence pastors spring. My sons, I do not promise
that you will renew the world. Ye will toil in the night
like Peter and his companions on the sea of Galilee,
without visible reward ; but in the end Christ will come,
and then will your gain be great. Be ye poor, live as
poor men, take not pleasure in titles nor in robes of

honour, neither in personal authority, neither in collective authority. Love those who hate you, hold yourselves aloof from parties. Make peace in the name of God ; accept not civil offices ; lord it not over souls nor seek to direct them over much ; do not force your priests like exotics in a hothouse; pray God that ye be many, but do not fear to be few ; do not suppose that you need much human knowledge, you need only much respect for reason and much faith in truth, which is universal and indivisible."

Such is the brotherhood to which the author of this remarkable novel would entrust the slow and patient preparation of his Christian Utopia. It is a sincere return to the spirit of the Gospel, a faithful attempt by one of the faithful to rouse the Church out of her self-satisfaction and recall her to the permanent conditions of the making of the Kingdom. It is a sign of the times to which even officialism dare not be blind; for in these days the novel is more powerful than even the most revolutionary theological treatise.

CHAPTER XII

THE PAPAL COMMISSION AND THE PENTATEUCH

THE Catholic Scientific Congress which met at Fribourg *February* in Switzerland in 1897, was an important event in the 1907 history of modern Catholicism. A note of vigorous life and confident sincerity pervaded its deliberations, especially with regard to Biblical questions ; and nowhere was that note more conspicuous than in the paper on the Hexateuch read by the Baron Friedrich von Hügel. But the Fribourg meeting had still more important consequences. When the Congress met again in 1900, the section dealing with Biblical questions had been suppressed by order of Leo XIII ; and two years later, on October 30th, 1902, a Special Commission was appointed by His Holiness to deal with the development of Biblical studies. The choice of Father David Fleming as Secretary of the Commission inspired Catholic scholars with confidence, and gave them a real hope that the questions raised by independent criticism would be honestly met. But all such hopes were rudely dispelled when, shortly after the accession of Pius X to the Papal Chair, Father Fleming was relieved of his duties on the Commission, and it seemed doubtful for a time whether the Commission itself would not be dissolved. However, another fate awaited it. What the scholars had hoped might prove a sympathetic or at least forbearing assessor of their labours was quickly turned, under reactionary

139

direction, into a scourge to reprove them withal. It is true that the Commission did not seem anxious to press matters immediately to a definite issue. As the *Tablet* of the 28th July last, when announcing the first really important decision of the Commission, somewhat naïvely but very accurately put it : " The Biblical Commission moves slowly—so slowly that its published decisions average rather less than one a year : the Biblical Commission is cautious—so cautious that hitherto its decisions have been little more than a succinct *negative* to certain theories advanced to solve some grave Biblical difficulties."

However, the oracle had at last spoken to some effect. It is an ancient merit in oracles that their answers be found flexible. Here, however, the answers were perfectly definite and unescapable. If the judgments of the Commission should at any future date require modification, occasion for it must be found in the carefully proposed questions to which its definite answers were given. It is already urged by some of those Catholic apologists who would like to stand equally well with the world of scholarship and the world of authority, that such opportunities of escape are in fact to be found in the form of the questions proposed. It is difficult, however, for the ordinary mind to discover the grounds of such a hope. That readers may form their own judgment, it may be well to quote the text of the questions as translated in the *Tablet* of July 28th, 1906 :—

" 1. Whether the arguments amassed by critics to impugn the Mosaic authenticity of the Sacred Books known as the Pentateuch are of sufficient weight, notwithstanding the very many evidences to the contrary contained in both Testaments taken collectively, the perpetual agreement of the Hebrew people, and the constant tradition of the Church as well as the proofs furnished by internal criticism of the text, to justify the statement that these books have not Moses for their author, but have been compiled from sources for the most part posterior to the time of Moses ?

"*Answer :* No.

" 2. Whether the Mosaic authenticity of the Pentateuch necessarily postulates a redaction of the whole work in the sense that it must be absolutely held that Moses wrote with his own hand or dictated to amanuenses all and everything contained in it ; or whether it is possible to admit the hypothesis of those who think that Moses conceived the work under the influence of divine inspiration, and then entrusted the writing of it to some other person or persons, but in such manner that they faithfully rendered his meaning, wrote nothing contrary to his will, and omitted nothing ; and that the work thus formed, approved by Moses as the principal and inspired author, was made public under his name ?

"*Answer :* No, to the first ; Yes, to the second.

" 3. Whether it can be conceded, without prejudice to the Mosaic authenticity of the Pentateuch, that Moses in his work used sources, *i.e.*, written documents or oral traditions, from which, to suit his special purpose and under the influence of Divine inspiration, he selected some things and inserted them in his own work, either verbally or in substance, summarised or amplified ?

"*Answer :* Yes.

"4. Whether, granted the substantial Mosaic authenticity and the integrity of the Pentateuch, it may be admitted that in the long course of ages some modifications have been introduced into it, such as additions after the death of Moses, either inserted by an inspired author or attached to the text as glosses or interpretations; words and forms translated from the ancient language to more recent languages; and finally, faulty readings to be ascribed to the error of amanuenses, concerning which it is lawful to investigate and judge according to the laws of criticism?

"*Answer :* Yes; due regard being paid to the judgment of the Church."

This decision, signed by the secretaries of the Commission, the Abbé Vigouroux and Dom Janssen, was reported to Pius X, who approved, and ordered its publication. Its present interest for us is that it has been the occasion of two excellent letters just published in a small volume by Longmans & Co., under the title, "The Papal Commission and the Pentateuch." The writers of these letters, it will be recognized by all, have a right to speak on the questions raised by the decision. In the first place, they are both Hebraists of undoubted competence. Dr. Briggs has attained a conspicuous place in the field of Biblical scholarship by his volume on the Hexateuch, and by his collaboration with Dr. Brown and Dr. Driver in the production of the new Hebrew Lexicon, in which " the uses of all Hebrew words in the Old Testament have been carefully examined and classified according to their historical development in the literature." More than that, he has suffered in the cause to which he has devoted a large share of the interest and activity of his life. It was ostensibly on account of his critical conclusions on Old Testament matters that he was expelled from the American Presbyterian Church, of which he was a member, by its General Assembly. The writer of the second letter in this little volume is Baron Friedrich von Hügel, to whose paper read before the Catholic Congress at Fribourg I have already referred. In the inner circle of international scholarship he is known as one of the soundest Hebraists and most fearless and competent critics now living.

But this is not the only, or even the chief, justification for their interference in the questions raised by the decisions of the Commission. It is undoubtedly open to any competent scholar to criticise these decisions on their merits. But to most scholars, if they are outside the Church of Rome or lacking in sympathy with it, the task of criticism other than the most perfunctory will no doubt have seemed superfluous, in any case futile, and perhaps even a little impertinent. It is not so with the writers of these letters. Dr. Briggs is known almost as much for his friendly attitude towards the Roman Church and for his ardent hopes and labours on behalf of the reunion of Christendom, as he is for his work as a Biblical scholar. And Baron von Hügel is a faithful son and devoted servant of the Roman Church. An interchange of views between two such men is of the first importance, and must, we should hope, command the respectful attention of the Roman authorities.

It is hardly necessary to enter here into the arguments which both these writers adduce against the indefensible position—at least from the point of view of criticism, the only one which has any claim to be considered in the question under discussion—assumed by the Commission. As Dr. Briggs succinctly puts it : " So far as the question of the Mosaic authorship of the Pentateuch is concerned, *that* has been settled in the arena of Biblical scholarship in the negative." And his arguments, arrayed notwithstanding their closeness with admirable clearness in a dozen pages, are reinforced by Baron von Hügel out of the abundance of his knowledge and his easy and thorough command of it. I would only say that, if anyone wishes to know what the expert has to say upon this matter, he cannot do better than read Dr. Briggs' letter in full, and the second part of the letter of Baron von Hügel. But it may, I think, be of even greater and more immediate interest to the ordinary reader to have his attention turned to the third part of the Baron's letter, in which he discusses the reasons for his hope that even " the immensely conservative Roman Catholic Church " may in time be led to accept and even to welcome the assured results of independent criticism.

" Four necessities," he says, " are working within Catholicism as such towards a final acceptance, however slow and cautious, of a consistent and sincere historico-critical method for the Bible." First of all, Catholicism, by its very character as a historical and institutional religion, " is wedded to history, and hence to historic proofs and methods." " It is, at bottom, a sheer logical impossibility, and a psychical condition of the most unstable equilibrium or sceptical effect, *both* to appeal to the facts, persons, and documents [associated with the

Christian tradition] as downrightly historical, *and* to refuse to submit them to thorough historical investigation." Secondly, Catholicism is a missionary religion, a religion that by its very nature must teach, and therefore must learn in order to teach. " For you cannot teach whom you do not understand, and you cannot win the man with whom you cannot share certain fundamental pre-suppositions." But in order to teach the educated West-European world of to-day, Catholicism must assimilate the intellectual temper of the cultivated non-Roman world which is, " in part unconsciously, often slowly yet everywhere surely, getting permeated and won by critical standards and methods. A system cannot both claim to teach all the world and erect an impenetrable partition-wall between itself and the educated portion of that world." Thirdly, Catholicism is essentially a " Church and Bible," not a " Bible only " religion. The old Protestant Bibliolatry is not Catholic, and Catholicism cannot afford to add to its intellectual difficulties and increase its intellectual burdens by an " un-Catholic super-exaltation of the Bible." And, finally, Catholicism is a growth, not a mere logical and analytical development of a fixed Revelation, but the dynamic development of a real spiritual life. " However rightly we may find a certain true uniqueness and the final norm for spiritual truth and practice in our Lord's Person, Life, and Teaching, and however legitimately we may talk of a period of Revelation followed by one of simple Assistance : there will, between Christ and His Spirit and the nowhere utterly God-forsaken world into which they have come, ever be a sufficient affinity for the former to be able to penetrate, appropriate, satisfy, and measure all the goodness, truth, and spiritual hunger variously yet ever present in the world. From Moses back to prehistoric times, forward to Christ, and on from Christ to the end of time, we thus get *one* great chain of slow, varying, intermittent, yet true development occasioned by God in man, and moving from man towards God. And if so, then the chief difficulty raised by the critical view of the various documents disappears : for such a truly dynamic conception would englobe and spiritualise it all."

And finally, the writer of this passionately felt and maturely conceived Christian Apologetic, for it is nothing less, turns to two considerations which may abate the ardour of the hope he has thus formed. Are there not signs that the line of cleavage in Christendom is coming to be lateral rather than horizontal, a cleavage occasioned and determined by different contemporary mentalities rather than by traditional confessional hostilities ? Are there not signs that the " traditionalists " of all confessions are drawing closely together to meet the attack of the " rationalists " of all confessions ? May not the Pope become the leader, actual if not recognized, of a crusade to rescue the Bible from the malevolence of the critics ? Against the possibility of such an alliance—and to many minds, and not the least far-seeing, it is a very real one—Baron von Hügel urges that "the immanental peculiarities of the Catholic position would soon break it up from the Roman side ; whilst on the Protestant side, even such strongly individualistic Bible-Protestants as the Congregationalists, the descendants of Cromwell and

Milton, are steadily maturing a critically-trained body of Ministers."

The second consideration is of more weight. It lies in the rigid attitude of Rome in the past on all matters which have become the object of a formal decision by her. "When and where has Rome quite finally abandoned any position, however informal and late its occupation, and however demonstrated its untenableness ?" And here the writer admits that he cannot fully arrest the blow. "Rome alone can do so, and not by words, but by deeds." However, he thinks he can break its force, and he proceeds to make the attempt by citing a number of instances, most of them from recent history, where, though Rome has not formally receded from untenable positions, has indeed in some cases quite recently occupied them, Roman scholars have with impunity not only abandoned them, but demonstrated their general untenableness. So then, he concludes, Rome may be, after all, more Catholic than she appears to be.

I have allowed Baron von Hügel to speak in the main for himself, first because I would not misrepresent him, and secondly, because he is one of those writers whose every word tells in that it has been wrung out of the total spiritual energy of the man. The letter which he has here written is not only a noble and quite unanswerable retort to an obscurantist decision, (obscurantist, I mean, as coming from a body of men professing to be scholars and to focus their scholarship upon a single question which has been minutely and with growing dispassionateness examined by the most capable expert students of the West during a hundred years) ; it is also, and especially that part of it with which I have mainly dealt, a magnificent contribution to that vital apologetic which Christianity demands at the present hour. Before leaving a plea for religious intelligence so entirely un- tainted by one trace of the cramping polemic which so often mars the words of even those writers on religious themes who would claim to be tolerant and impartial, yet so rooted in devotion to the Roman Church, I would quote still another passage which it will be well for us all to ponder. Personal as it is, perhaps because personal, it ought to be a word of general and magnificent inspira- tion. "Born in Florence, my imagination was early impressed with the great figures of Dante and of Savonarola, and, later on, by those of Marsilio Ficino and his fellow Platonizers. The spacious outlook and virile depth and tenacity of that early Catholic Renais- sance still fire my blood ; neither Protestantism as such (so pathetically understandable, yet so largely unjust because ungenerous), nor a bitter, puny anti-Protestant- ism, a Catholicism contracted to a mere negation of negations, or to a system of the greatest possible ex- clusion of trouble, trial, and danger can (so all my being tells me) be the final, God-willed solution for all the battles, heroisms, faults, sins, and glories of so many centuries of Western Christendom."

CHAPTER XIII

M. LE ROY ON THE NATURE OF DOGMA

THE appearance of M. Le Roy in the field of theological 1907 controversy was a notable event in the history of the Liberal Catholic movement. M. Le Roy, as all readers of the *Revue de Métaphysique et de Morale* will know, is a philosopher of assured competence, a distinguished representative of the later French school whose chief masters are M. Henri Bergson and M. Émile Boutroux. He is also a devout and " practising " Catholic layman. Two years ago—in April, 1905, to be exact—he published in the *Quinzaine* an article in which he put and attempted a reply to the question—" What is a dogma ? " The article provoked a ferment of discussion which has not even yet subsided. M. Le Roy has at length collected a number of the replies to the criticism which was directed against him from the orthodox camp, and has published them along with his original article in a volume of nearly 400 pages, entitled " Dogme et Critique." The book forms perhaps the most important contribution of our time to the discussion of the nature of dogma. Yet, intensely modern as is its point of view, it but carries on the almost uniform tradition of mystical theology, and more especially the tradition of the Seraphic Doctor and his later disciples. It is interesting to find a seventeenth century disciple of Duns Scotus, Frassen, using such words as these :—" Our theology is not scientific knowledge. It is by no means speculative, but directly practical. The object of theological knowledge does not exist to be thought discursively, but to be wrought actively."* Here is the whole philosophy of the " primacy of action " already applied to the conception of dogma.

I

It may be well to confine our exposition of M. Le Roy's argument within the framework provided by his examination of the question in the original *Quinzaine* article. Here he divides his subject into two parts. In the first he demonstrates the impossibility of commending the ordinary intellectualist conception of dogma to modern ways of thinking. The second he devotes to a positive exposition of the nature of dogma, such as will both preserve its real religious value and gain acceptance for it with the thinker of to-day.

We have passed, says M. Le Roy, beyond the stage of partial and particular heresies. That stage was possible only so long as there was agreement between the defenders of orthodoxy and their heretical opponents on the first principles of all discussion. Such agreement no longer exists. The modern thinker does not reject this dogma or that, founding his rejection on arguments drawn from first principles held in common by himself and his orthodox antagonist. He rejects the very idea of dogma, and that for four reasons. In the first place, a dogma claims to be a truth given on mere external authority.

* Theologia nostra non est scientia . . . Nostra theologia nullatenus speculativa est, sed simpliciter practica . . . Theologiæ objectum non est speculabile, sed operabile.

Those who assert its truth not only deny the necessity, but even affirm the impossibility, of demonstrating that truth intrinsically. Now it is the first necessity of modern thought to find even for its most fundamental axioms some basis of certainty, if only by demonstrating that those axioms are necessary conditions of knowledge, certainties implied in every activity of the reason. It owes all its success to its keeping in closest touch with fact and requiring clear and unmistakable proof for every detailed conclusion. The very idea, therefore, of the strictly dogmatic proposition is wholly repugnant to it. And in the most important matters of knowledge it rightly requires the clearest and most unambiguous proof, while it is just in these matters that it is asked to believe on the naked assurance of authority.

But here the traditional apologist may reply that a dogma is by no means given without proof. He admits that he is unable to establish the how and the why of any dogmatic truth whatsoever. Yet he claims to establish its truth none the less, and points to the analogy of the physicist who has often to accept facts which he cannot theoretically explain, or to that of the historian who has to accept all his knowledge on external evidence. But it is evident that the analogy will not hold good. For the physicist is compelled to accept facts which elude his theory, just because they are facts of his immediate knowledge, facts disclosed by minute observation and exact experiment. But the facts which dogma asserts can make no claim to be facts of this kind. Again, it is true that the historian gains all his knowledge on the evidence of others. But he admits the facts of such knowledge exactly because they are facts of which in like circumstances he has himself had direct experience. In proportion as the reported facts are remote from the facts of his own experience, either by distance in time or by dissimilarity in their character and connection, it is more difficult for him to give them credence or to accept them as genuine. And here, again, the analogy tells against and not for the truth of dogma in the mind of the thinker who has had a modern training. For the facts to which dogma witnesses are exactly of that disconcerting and mysterious kind which would require overwhelming evidence for their acceptance.

It is clear, then, that these pretended proofs of dogmatic propositions have no demonstrative validity. They rest inevitably upon the appeal to mere authority. And here is another reason for the rejection of the very idea of dogma by the modern mind. It cannot endure the imposition of truth upon the mind from without. It cannot even conceive the possibility of truth so enforced. For it truth is the process of development of something already given in the mind, of some inherent principle of order or need of growth adapting itself to, and so assimilating to itself, the facts of experience. " No truth," as M. Le Roy puts it, " can enter into us except it is postulated by something which precedes it as its more or less necessary complement, just as food in order to become effective nourishment supposes in him who receives it certain preliminary dispositions and preparations, viz., the call of hunger and the power of digestion. Even the establishment of a scientific fact presents this characteristic, since no fact has any meaning and therefore any existence for us except in virtue of some theory out of which it issues as a fact of our knowledge, and into which as a fact of our knowledge it fits." So then the attempt to establish truth by considerations and arguments extrinsic to the truth itself is radically opposed to the spirit, the attitude, and the method of modern thought.

But in spite of all this, let us concede to authority the right to teach truths by a simple affirmation which no one has a corresponding right to criticise. In that case it might legitimately be claimed that the truths taught should have a clear and unmistakable meaning. But so far is this from being the case with regard to religious dogmas that their formulas are often couched in the language of a philosophic system which it is no longer easy even for the trained philosopher to understand, and which is not free from the danger of suggesting equivocal and even contradictory meanings. " The doctrine of the Word, for instance, has close bonds of attachment with Alexandrian Neo-Platonism, while the theory of matter and form in the Sacraments, or that of the relations between substance and accidents in the dogma of the Real Presence are closely allied to Aristotelian and scholastic conceptions. Now, these different philosophies are sometimes doubtful as to their basis and obscure in expression. In any case they have long since become obsolete, and are no longer in use among philosophers and scholars. To be a Christian, then, must one begin by getting converted to these philosophies ? An enterprise so exacting that many a believer would find himself singularly embarrassed in presence of it ! And besides, even that would not be sufficient, for the medley of several languages, having their origin in conflicting philosophies, constitutes still another difficulty even more troublesome than the former." But M. Le Roy points out that the confusion as to the meaning of dogmatic statements does not end here. For many of the terms which they employ are not even borrowed from philosophies of the past, but are simple metaphors borrowed from common sense—such as the Divine Fatherhood or the Divine Sonship. Now it is clearly impossible to give a precise intellectual meaning to these metaphors and so to fix their theoretical value. As M. Le Roy says :—" They are images inconvertible into concepts." And so the confusion is increased by the mixture of these imaginative symbols with the abstract philosophic formulas of which we have already spoken. A third cause, therefore, of the rejection of dogmas by the contemporary mind is that they offer it no meaning which can be thought out. M. Le Roy quotes a saying of M. Belot :—" The most embarrassing requirement which could be made of the generality of believers would be that, before they were asked at all for a proof of what they believe, they should define exactly what it is that they affirm and deny."

But again, the contemporary mind rejects the idea of dogma as a system of intellectual truth, because it is useless and unfruitful. It does not fit in with the knowledge which the modern mind is most confident of possessing, so as to form with it a coherent body of truth. Because it is unchangeable, it remains alien to that progress which is the very essence of truth. Because it

is transcendent, it has no relations with the effective life
of the intellect. This, says M. Le Roy, is the gravest
reproach which can be levelled against it at a moment
" when it is more and more clearly perceived that the
value of a truth is measured before everything else by
the services which it renders, by the new results which
it suggests, by the consequences with which it is
pregnant ; in short, by the vivifying influence which it
exercises over the whole body of knowledge."

II

It will be seen that what M. Le Roy shows to be anti-
pathetic to modern thought is not dogma itself, but the
particular conception of dogma which is current in the
orthodox apologetic. He holds, therefore, that this
intellectualist conception is not, and cannot be, the true
Catholic conception. But before going on to consider
what conception of dogma is possible which will commend
to the modern mind the reality to which dogma witnesses,
let us examine by particular instances whether the
intellectualist conception does in fact justify the claim
which it makes. That conception is that dogma is the
enunciation of a truth of the speculative or theoretical
order, without any demonstration and on the mere word
of authority. Every dogma ought, therefore, to be a
distinct and appreciable addition to the sum of our
knowledge. Let us examine, then, from this point of
view the dogma of the Personality of God. What
distinct idea, having its place and effect in the order of
our theoretical knowledge, is conveyed to us by the statement that God is personal ? If the word is used to suggest

to us that the Divine nature is but a kind of idealization of the human nature which we know, that it is but that nature exalted to its perfect expression, then we are landed in an anthropomorphism which Catholic theologians would be the first to reject. If, on the other hand, personality is used of the Divine nature to indicate its incomparable and transcendent excellence, its use can only create illusion. While suggesting something which we know, it is employed to indicate something which, it is implied, we cannot know. Here no truth of the speculative or theoretical order, and destined to be fruitful in that order, has been conveyed to us. As M. Le Roy admirably puts it :—" Either we define personality and fall inevitably into anthropomorphism ; or we do not define it, and fall no less inevitably into agnosticism."

Or again, let us take the dogma of the Resurrection of Jesus. If the purpose of this dogma is to add to our knowledge by guaranteeing to us the exact manner in which a certain fact was accomplished, if it is a statement having its place in the intellectual order, then we must first ask ourselves what is implied by the word " resurrection." Does that word imply that after three days Jesus reappeared in the same life-conditions as those which had governed His earthly life ? The Gospels themselves expressly state the contrary. "The idea represented by the word ' life ' has not, then, the same content when we apply it to the period which preceded the Crucifixion and to that which followed it. What, then, does it represent when applied to this second period ? Nothing which can be expressed in an intellectual concept." Here, as in the case of personality, another word ought to be adopted whose application might be reserved to the unique case to which alone it corresponds.

Or again, let us take the dogma of the Real Presence. A being is ordinarily said to be present only when it can be perceived or manifests itself through perceptible effects. Now the dogma itself denies both these characters to the Presence which it affirms. That Presence is mysterious and unique, and its manner is not in the slightest degree conveyed, at least as an addition to our theoretical knowledge, by the use of that word. So the conception of dogmas as statements communicating to us theoretical knowledge breaks down at every point.

But these very instances which we have chosen may suggest to us a truer conception of the nature of dogma. The dogma of the Personality of God may not add to our speculative knowledge of the nature of God ; but it serves to direct that practical knowledge of Him which is the only knowledge that religion is concerned with. It says in effect to us :—" Conduct yourselves in your relations with God as you would in your relations with a human person." In the same way, the dogma of the Resurrection of Jesus does not add to our knowledge of the new life which Jesus lived after death or to the manner of the transformation of the old life into the new. But it says to us :—" Let your relations to Him now be what they would have been before His death, or what they are to your own contemporaries." And again, the dogma of the Real Presence conveys to us no knowledge of the modality of that presence. But it enjoins upon us the necessity of preserving in the presence of the consecrated Host such an attitude of spirit as we should feel in the presence of Jesus Himself if He were visible to us.

Dogmas, then, are primarily rules of practical conduct, practical guides to the spirit and conduct of the religious life. Their value is religious and not speculative. And that this must be the prerogative character of dogma will be evident when we reflect that Christianity is not a speculative philosophy, but " a source and a rule of life, a discipline of moral and religious action." The intellectualist, indeed, does not deny this practical character of dogma, but he insists that it is secondary and derived. For him dogma is primarily a revelation adding to our speculative knowledge, and just because it is so can make and enforce its practical claims upon life. He places theology before religion, and makes the latter depend upon the former. But in so doing he reverses the actual order of life. For the propositions of dogma are not within the comprehension of most of those who have led, or are leading, the Christian life with a steadfast faithfulness and loyalty. And that is to grant what we have seen cannot be granted, that they are comprehensible propositions at all in the sense of additions to or developments of our theoretical knowledge. The intellectualist, therefore, would make the religious life depend upon the prior enunciation and acceptance of unintelligible propositions. But let us accept dogma as fitted to man's practical needs, and its propositions are by no means unintelligible. For then all its metaphors drawn from the language of common sense, its anthropomorphic symbols and analogies, are full of force and meaning. The dogmatic proposition exists for man and his religious life, and therefore naturally and rightly clothes itself in language drawn from the most intimate and vital human relations and experiences.

But it may be urged that such a conception of dogma altogether separates our knowledge of God from that supreme expression of human life—the life of thought. No consequence of such a conception could be more unwarranted. And indeed, the need of some reconciliation between the life of thought and the nature of dogma so conceived arises immediately out of the conception itself. For, it may be urged, if the voice of authority is not justified in uttering dogmas which have a theoretical import, how is it any the more justified in teaching dogmas of practical import only ? The necessity of an appeal to the reason at once declares itself. And the answer which reason itself gives is that there is no authority which can impose speculative truth, but that there is an authority whose very function it is to direct conduct and the life of the spirit which expresses itself in conduct. And the Church is just such an authority. For the Church is above everything else the generalised tradition of the highest religious experience. From that character of hers proceeds all her authority. By the degree in which she preserves that character and makes it effectual, the total economy of her authority and all her authoritative action must be judged. The modern mind may still criticise this use of the Church's authority, but it will not challenge as irrational her right to its use.

But again, there is a necessary relation between dogmas and thought. For thought is involved in all action. It

is impossible to act save under the guidance of some kind
of vague diffused light. We choose our path because of
some sufficient light which determines the choice. The
light that guides us is not of course the light of discursive
reason. That is a light which would not so much guide as
compel. But there is what we call the experience of life,
which is but the operation of thought in all our actions.
And so we do not accept dogmas blindly. We accept
them because of their rational conformity with experience.
Whereas, if they were indeed what the intellectualist
represents them to be, revelations of speculative truth,
they would compel our acceptance, they would render
impossible that act of faith which is rooted in the freedom
of the will and which theology itself asserts to be the only
method of their acceptance.

And again, it is because dogmas have a practical aim
that they can claim in a very real sense, in the only
admissible sense, to be unchangeable. For the practical
life is uniform in its motives and texture, and therefore
appeals to it can preserve the same meaning for all. If
dogmas had primarily an intellectual character, and so
far as they had that character, they would necessarily
convey a different meaning in different ages and to men
of different intellectual culture. But it is the very claim
of religion that they should always and everywhere make
the same effectual appeal, and that is only possible when
they are conceived of as primarily rules of life.

But dogmas have a still closer connection with thought.
For, however practical their immediate import, they
witness to a world of unseen reality with which they
desire to bring our action into relation. And we cannot

help thinking of that world of reality as best we can, and bringing it into ordered intellectual relation with the rest of our knowledge. We are forced to form images of that world whereby it may correspond with and fit into the framework of our other knowledge. These systems of images and analogies constitute those theological constructions which have succeeded each other throughout the Christian ages. So it is that theology grows out of religion, that the speculative element of dogma is secondary and not primary, that the activity of the discursive reason in framing dogmatic statements is subsequent to those affirmations of faith in which nevertheless the reason inherent in every act of life is implied.

But finally, M. Le Roy holds that there is an immediate speculative import in dogma. Yet even that import is determined by its practical character. He insists that every dogma has at least a *negative* value in the order of speculative thought. If it does not positively determine truth, at least it excludes and condemns certain positions as erroneous. For instance, if it asserts that God is personal, it teaches nothing explicit about this personality, it does not reveal its nature or provide any precise idea of it. But it denies " that God is a mere law, a formal category, an ideal principle, an abstract entity, a universal substance, or some cosmic force diffused throughout the universe." In the same way the dogma of the Resurrection of Jesus does not reveal the means by which that unique fact was accomplished or the nature of Christ's second life. But it denies that His death set a term to His action upon the world. And it denies, too, that His present action upon the world is similar to that of some dead-and-gone thinker whose influence remains living and fruitful, and whose work is followed by long-continued effects. Again, the dogma of the Real Presence enunciates no theory of that Presence, nor even teaches us in what it consists. But it warns us that the Presence is not to be understood in certain ways, that, for example, the consecrated Host must not be held to be merely a figure or symbol of Jesus. It is evident how this negative significance of dogma is determined by and complementary to its positive practical character. It is just the danger to its practical and directive import that has in fact always motived, and can alone justify, its negative witness in the sphere of speculative thought.

M. Le Roy sums up his argument in two propositions :—

1. The intellectualist conception which is current to-day renders insoluble most of the objections provoked by the idea of dogma.

2. The doctrine of the primacy of action, on the contrary, provides for a solution of the problem without sacrificing either the rights of thought or the requirements of dogma.

PART II

Facts and Forces

CHAPTER I

THE FRENCH ELECTIONS OF 1902

M. WALDECK-ROUSSEAU may return to his practice at June, 1902 the Bar and escape definitely from the dust of the political arena. But, none the less, he will remain one of the three great statesmen of the Third Republic. With Gambetta and Ferry he will rank as its saviour in a time of crisis. Since the crisis, forced by the letter of MacMahon which dissolved the ministry of Jules Simon on the famous Seize Mai in the year 1877, the Republic has known no such peril, not even in the mad days of Boulangism, as that which it had to face in the darkness and confusion of the terrible Dreyfus struggle of 1899. When on the 22nd of June in that year the new President of the Council attempted, amid a scene of indescribable tumult which can be but dimly realized by those who read the report in the *Journal Officiel*, to explain his programme to the Chamber of Deputies, it seemed impossible to hope that his Ministry would last longer or be more successful than that of his immediate predecessors. Yet he carried Revision, brought back the poor prisoner of the Devil's Isle and set him before his new judges at Rennes, granted him a free pardon when he had been once more condemned, and stanched the wounds of a lacerated France by the act of general amnesty. The work of Republican defence seemed to be complete, and all the voices of reaction called for the

165

resignation of the Minister whose mandate was, according to them, exhausted. But he himself interpreted his duty otherwise. The work of Republican defence involved, in his opinion, a development of Republican activity. He threw down the gauntlet to the Clerical party in the Associations Law of last July. It was a bold, some thought a rash and even suicidal, move. There was a wild scramble of all the forces of reaction to pick it up. Under the standard of the " Ligue de la patrie française," which M. Anatole France has called with mordant wit the " Ligue de la patrie romaine," the reaction marshalled its forces confident of victory. Had not the Angel Gabriel appeared in a village of Touraine to the prophetic child, Mdlle. Couesdon, and announced the victory of the Nationalists in heavenly verses ? Had not pious ladies stinted themselves of legitimate social pleasures, abandoned their dances and receptions throughout the winter, that they might fill the electoral war-chest ? And the result has been that on the clearest issue on which an election has been fought in the history of the Third Republic, the reaction has been hopelessly beaten. M. Waldeck-Rousseau's Government has a clear majority of close upon a hundred over the combined forces of Royalists, Ralliés, Nationalists, and anti-Ministerial Republicans. The Republican Concentration, for which the *Temps* timorously clamoured in the weeks before the election, has become so unnecessary that even that careful journal no longer refers to it. The new President of the Council, whoever he may be, whether M. Waldeck-Rousseau or M. Barthou or M. Doumer or another, can count on a clear majority of the Left without turning a wistful eye to the benches occupied by MM. Méline, Ribot, Poincaré, and Aynard.

Now much as English Liberals, and indeed Englishmen generally, may rejoice over this victory of the Left, there is something about it which must sadden and disturb us. For it is essentially a victory of Anti-Clericalism. At first sight, indeed, that need not disturb us at all. It ought to be but one reason the more for profound satisfaction with the result. The use of the organized forces of the Church for mere political wreckage, any attempt on the part of the Church to determine the form of State organization, is a prostitution of its sacred functions, for which it deserves whatever punishment it may incur. And that is, unfortunately, the part which the Church has consistently played since the proclamation of the Third Republic. She has shrunk from no alliance, however incongruous, she has recoiled from no stratagem, however mean and unworthy, if haply she might maim the existing Constitution. It was her action in the crisis of the Seize Mai that drove Gambetta into the declaration that clericalism was the enemy—a declaration which has ever since been the touchstone of Republican policy. But Anti-Clericalism had become distinctly less virulent, it had spent its force and relapsed into the impotence of a traditional shibboleth, during the Nineties. A wise Church could have exorcised that evil spirit. Never had there been such an opportunity of doing so. The Pope had wisely called upon French Catholics to rally to the Republic—only, we are told, to rouse the pious ladies of Royalist households to pray for his conversion. The intellect of France had been turning with sympathy, and

its heart with yearning, to the old truths and hopes of the
Christian religion.   The foremost names in literary France,
men like M. Coppée and M. Brunetière and M. Bourget,
were rallying to the Church.   But to the Old Guard they
remained suspect, barely tolerated.   The secret distrust
with which they were regarded, in spite of the political
apostasy to which many of them were ready to commit
themselves in the supposed interests of their recovered
faith, found open expression some months ago in the
manifesto of the honest and straightforward, if distinctly
reactionary, Mgr. Turinaz, Bishop of Nancy—"Les
Périls de la foi et de la discipline dans l'église française."
Every advantage which the Church had in the changed
spirit of the time she seemed anxious to reject or annul.
And then came her crowning opportunity and her great
refusal—the "affaire Dreyfus."   It seemed almost
designed to be the touchstone of the zeal for righteousness,
or call it mere fair play, of every corporate unity in the
life of France.   And the only thing it proved with regard
to the Church was her blindness of heart or her readiness
to turn the sacred cause of justice into a weapon of
political attack, her moral indifference or her immoral
chicane.   It would be difficult to decide which is the more
charitable account of her action were it not only too
clear that all charity is forbidden, and that her attitude
revealed both the one and the other.   She stirred into a
loathly and poisonous life in the national breast what
M. Anatole Leroy-Beaulieu, himself a faithful son of the
Church and one of those moderate Liberals who do honour
to France, has well called "les doctrines de haine."
Through the veins of France there ran once more the fiery

poison of Anti-Semitism and Anti-Protestantism. And the Church cannot be relieved of the odium of having deliberately inoculated the nation, and of all the bitter consequences which even yet that action may entail. Two, at least, of her most powerful Congregations, to which were committed the greatest influence for good or for evil which any body can enjoy, the influence of the School and the influence of the Press, stand condemned in the judgment of the plain practical man—the Jesuits and the Assumptionists. One might have hoped that the Christian School would have justified itself by the presence of some instinct for justice in its former pupils. One might have hoped that a Christian Press would have evinced a more worthy temper than the violence and insanity of the *Croix*. The tragedy of the present situation in France is that the Church seems anxious to prove even to the most patient of the *bien pensants* that which a hostile world had already proclaimed to be beyond all need of proof—her constitutional incapacity to understand the modern spirit, to discipline and control it in those permanent interests of humanity which are always spiritual. During a whole decade she had an unexampled opportunity, alike in the growing goodwill of the best representatives of the modern spirit and in the insensible alleviation of the hatred with which she had been undoubtedly menaced, of learning and answering to the claims which the time made upon her. But she has absolutely refused to learn. Her only answer to the spirit of the new age has been an uncompromising anathema. It seems as though she had deliberately sought to justify and accentuate the suspicion with which the Revolution spirit regarded her by launching against it a declaration of irreconcilable enmity. She might have revealed to its confident and heady materialism its fatal insufficiency, she might have tempered it with a sense of spiritual possibility and moral purpose, if she had only come out into the open and met it on equal terms. But she chose instead to ban it from the spiritual twilight of the sacristy. She might have humanised and touched to issues of spiritual fruitfulness its somewhat abstract and barren idealism. But she chose instead to curse it altogether as a fatal and Satanic delusion. On the side of positive action the France of the Revolution, and especially of the Third Republic, has unfortunately only known the Church as a wily and implacable enemy incessantly working for its destruction by underhand diplomacy and crooked intrigue. Her very virtues have made her suspect with the Republic, since they have been consistently directed to its ruin. The self-sacrifice, the devotion, the unexampled charity of Catholic France are but one menace the more for Republican France. The zeal of the teaching orders, of the Christian Brothers and the Jesuit Fathers, is quite legitimately dreaded by the authority which guides the State. It is always unconsciously, even when it is not deliberately, directed to undermining the principles on which the State rests.

This is an impossible attitude save on one assumption—viz., that the modern spirit is really an inspiration of Satan. In that case the Church of France is magnificently and heroically in the right, except indeed in so far as she condescends to fight the spiritual enemy with weapons of his own forging. And that unfortunately must be, in any case, a very considerable modification of the respect which her uncompromising opposition to the false gods of the State might otherwise inspire. But if she is right, then the Christianity of England, of America, and of Germany are hopelessly wrong. Their patient and tempered optimism, their readiness to make the best of the world as it is and to refuse to take up their abode in the charnel-house of the past, are but the evidences of a cowardly and compromising spirit or of an incurable spiritual blindness. And if she is right and they are wrong, then religion is doomed. Religion itself is the enemy in the victorious path of the materialistic spirit incarnate in the modern State. That is, unfortunately, the conclusion at which the anti-clerical temper in France has arrived. Anti-clericalism has become, and the attitude of the Church has forced it to become, anti-Christianity, even anti-Theism. It is against the religious spirit itself that an increasing number of French electors vote, because for them the religious spirit is the monopoly of that Church which is the irreconcilable enemy of every ideal they cherish. There are few things more significant than the rout of the Abbés in the late elections. Wherever they stood, in the Creuse, in the Isère, in the Lot, in the Meurthe et Moselle, in the Maine et Loire, they have been defeated, and, as a rule, defeated by enormous majorities. Only at Hazebrouck, in the Nord, was the Abbé Lemire, the " heretic of the *Soutane* " and Christian Democrat, unassailable even by the Church which suspects him. The Abbé Gayraud, who alone is like-minded with him, had actually to face a clerical enemy, the Abbé Stéphan, in the Catholic constituency of Brest—only, however, to prove the weakness of the official opposition of the Church to her own large-hearted and clear-sighted children.

The tragedy of the situation is that liberty itself is in danger, that liberty indeed cannot exist in the midst of the civil war to which France is a prey—the war between two ideals which refuse to meet, and yet in whose reconciliation is the only hope for her future. It is quite possible that the triumphant Left may think the time opportune for annulling the last guarantees of the Loi Falloux for liberty of teaching, may restore the monopoly of the University, may make it illegal for the Congregations to teach. No greater disaster could overtake France, for then religion would disappear as an element in moulding her future. But if by any evil fortune the liberalism of the Charter of 1830 should at last founder, the Church must herself bear a very large share of the responsibility for a veritable spiritual catastrophe. Even yet she has the chance of abandoning her intransigent attitude of learning nothing and unlearning nothing. There are not wanting perhaps signs that she is still capable of the supreme virtue of teachableness. The Dominicans produced the greatest Catholic Liberal of the last half of the nineteenth century, the late Père Didon, and though they did not treat him too well, they seem at least to have acquired something of his liberal temper. They are now among the authorised Congregations under the new law. There is surely, too, reason, and very great reason, for hopefulness in the changed theological temper of the School of the New Apologetic, the school against which the fury of the traditional scholasticism has flung with perfect justice what it considers as the damning epithet of Kantism. Yet it can afford to be complacent under the bitterest attacks, for has it not as its chief patrons the enlightened Archbishop of Albi, Mgr. Mignot, and the Bishop of La Rochelle, Mgr. Le Camus, who has revised on modern lines the theological teaching of his diocesan seminary? With such forces at work, it is not too much to hope that the Church of France may yet at the eleventh hour be able and willing to undertake that task of reconciliation which is, in virtue of her Divine mission, peculiarly her own.

CHAPTER II

THE NEW APOLOGETIC IN FRANCE

August, In the French Church Liberalism has been sporadic
1902 throughout the whole course of the century which has
just ended. But its fortunes have been varied rather
than happy. It is a little disquieting to those of us who
are following with a sympathetic interest the latest of
these movements to recall the fate of its predecessors.
We remember the fate of that little band of distinguished
Liberal Catholics who wrought something greater than
they knew, who dealt a fatal blow to the last remains of
the old Gallican liberties, and established in the Church
of France the Ultramontanism which crushed its authors.
We remember the greatness of soul, the austere saintliness,
of the excommunicated Lamennais. We remember
Gratry, Perreyve, Montalembert. We remember with
mixed feelings of admiration and pity Lacordaire, who
was not strong enough to stand by the friend who had
inspired all that was best in him when that friend was
placed under the Church's ban, but who closed a career
of pathetic disillusion with the words on his lips :—
" I die a penitent Catholic, but an impenitent Liberal."

The Liberal movement had perished by the instrument
which it had so elaborately forged. Independence of
thought and of action seemed to have vanished from
the Church which had been its chosen home. Yet it
had not utterly disappeared. Again we remember

174

Mgr. d'Hulst, Lenormant, the Abbé de Broglie. Above all we remember the sublime figure of the second great Dominican of the century, Père Didon. We have been reminded by those exquisite letters which have just appeared,* of the exile of Corbara, of the great spirit who could appreciate so fully from the heart of an alien communion the religious sincerity and greatness of Germany, who detected unerringly the sources of religious weakness in his own land, and devoted the closing years of his life in a spirit of patient courage and faith to a humble attempt at their removal.

And now once more the Liberal movement has declared itself—this time decisively in the sphere of dogma. During the past decade the breath of a new life has been stirring among the dry bones of the old theology, till at last they have begun to move as living forms, invoking the attention of all those who are interested in such resurrection. Religious thought in France is fast coming into line with those developments which have been long familiar to us in the theology of Germany, Scotland, America, and England. And what is most interesting and hopeful in this change is that it is by no means confined to academic circles. It has its representatives among bishops ruling great dioceses and humble parish priests or country curates absorbed in the constant round of pastoral work, as well as among seminary professors and the occupants of chairs in Catholic Faculties. The protagonist of this movement, which calls itself the " New Apologetic," but which we may more intelligibly, if less accurately, name the " New Theology," is an Archbishop

* In the *Revue des Deux Mondes*, Jan. and Feb., 1902.

—Mgr. Mignot, the Archbishop of Albi, a diocese made famous (or infamous) in the history of the thirteenth century by the relentless crusade of Simon de Montfort and his Dominican allies against its heretical inhabitants, and possessing a certain interest, even in the twentieth century, through having for its representative in the Chamber of Deputies the great Socialist tribune and orator, M. Jaurès. And Mgr. Mignot is by no means the only Bishop whose name is prominently associated with the "New Theology." Mgr. Le Camus, the newly-appointed Bishop of La Rochelle (another historic stronghold of heresy—this time that of the sixteenth century) has had the courage to remodel the teaching of his diocesan seminary and to abandon the sacred tradition of scholasticism in the training of the future priests of his diocese. Many other Bishops are credited with an affection for the new learning, among them Mgr. Servonnet, the Archbishop of Bourges, Mgr. Lacroix, Bishop of Tarentaise, and Mgr. Fuzet, Archbishop of Rouen. But at least they have not declared themselves so definitely as Mgr. Mignot by his discourse on the Method of Theology or Mgr. Le Camus by his revolutionary change in the instrument of seminarist study.

To those who think of Roman theological science as being mainly a study of the catalogues of fossilized dogmas carefully arranged by the great systematisers of the past, the originality, the freshness, the variety of contemporary French theology will probably be a surprise. Of course it is proverbially difficult for the outsider to estimate aright the real force of movements which to him present a show of strength. Boldness or even violence in

innovation may often go with, may often be accounted
for by, a contemptuous indifference or a serene and
unregarding assurance on the part of established beliefs.
But there are many signs that the New Theology in
France is not only very much in earnest itself, but is also
being taken seriously by those who dislike and fear it.
The alarm has been sounded throughout France in notes
of passionate violence and obstinate conviction from the
mouth of Mgr. Turinaz, the vigorous Bishop of Nancy.
The local organs of religious opinion, the " Semaines
Religieuses " of the different dioceses, ring with the
clamour of battle and strain at the grim work of attack
and defence.   The epithets of " Protestant " and
" Kantian " are flung about in the most promiscuous
fashion.   Theological journals like the *Annales de
Philosophie Chrétienne*, or the *Revue du Clergé
Français*, which are widely read among the scholarly
members of the French clergy—and the interest in
scholarship is much more widely diffused throughout
that body than we imagine—open their columns freely
to able champions of the new movement.   Indeed, the
editors of these journals, the Abbé Denis and the Abbé
Bricout, are themselves among its ablest representatives.
Then again it is a fact of no small moment in estimating
the force of this movement that members of the great
religious orders like the Dominicans and the Jesuits, who
would be the first to feel the constraints of religious
expediency, are among the leading advocates and
practicians of the new theological method.   This very
trustworthy religious barometer seems to be at " set fair,"
though one must admit that its changes are often

unexpected and even unaccountable. Lastly, the readiness of the new theology to come out into the open and lean for philosophic support upon the writings, not only of Catholic laymen like M. Fonsegrive and M. Brunetière, but also of non-Catholics like M. Bergson and M. Boutroux, has already attracted to it the sympathetic attention of many thoughtful Frenchmen who have not hitherto evinced much interest in religious questions.

It would be obviously impossible to achieve and presumptuous to attempt even in outline an account of such a movement in the space of one short article—nor indeed am I anxious to make the attempt. I should be satisfied if I could persuade my fellow-countrymen and fellow-churchmen that on the other side of the Channel as here, in the heart of Roman orthodoxy as with us, the real difficulties which sincere religious thinkers have to face are difficulties in the interpretation of that deposit of traditional Christian teaching which we call dogma, and that the method of meeting those difficulties with some hope of success is gradually becoming one and the same throughout the whole area of Western Christendom. Perhaps I can best do this by selecting at random a few examples of the way in which the theological problems that clamour for solution are being met by contemporary French theologians. Let us take, to begin with, the origin and the nature of the difficulty. For to understand the origin of a difficulty is to be well on the way towards a recognition of its nature. I have seldom read a more frank and lucid exposition of the origin of the modern theological problem than that given by a writer in the current number of the *Revue du Clergé*

Français.   He reminds us that up to the close of the
Middle Age, and even later, all human knowledge,
whether religious or secular, started from exactly the
same premisses.   If the science of those days reached
slightly different conclusions on particular points from
received theological teaching, such difference occasioned
no alarm, as the ultimate data of both science and
religion remained the same.   The idea of a science
independent of Scripture was entertained no more
at Wittemberg than at Rome till near the close of
the seventeenth century.   To-day the aspect of their
relations is entirely changed.   A scientist may be Christian
or unbeliever, but his science is equally independent of
all theological assumptions.   To realize the nature and
extent of this change it is necessary to remember two
things—the new method of scientific knowledge, and the
actual conclusions to which it has led.   Science was
once a rigorous deduction from certain preliminary truths
as to the origin and nature of the world which were taken
as revealed.   It is now the gradual elaboration of general
views of the process by which the world's life is developing,
founded upon the patient and unprejudiced observation
of facts.   Formerly the man of science started from the
revealed certainty of how things began, and accommodated
as skilfully as he could the facts of his own experience and
observation to that indisputable certainty.   Now he
begins just with the facts that he can observe, and seeks
back to some working theory which will account for
them.   And as to the conclusions of the new scientific
method, how far they have removed our knowledge of
nature from the old theological hypotheses !   Then " the

universe was of recent origin, small in extent, and destined to be short-lived. The earth was its centre, not only because the sun and a number of tiny stars moved round it, but because it alone was inhabited, because the eye of God was fixed upon it only, and because by the Incarnation He had raised human nature to a level with His own. There was no science save that of God and of man in relation to God, and this science was contained in its entirety in infallible books preserved by an infallible Church." Now " the limits of space and time have been thrown back immeasurably. The universe is not a sphere whose form and movement the eye can easily take in. The earth is not its centre. All that is mere appearance. The earth is a humble satellite of a star which is itself but a grain of dust in immensity. It did not issue from nothingness six thousand years ago. Ascend some high mountain peak, take a block of the marble you may find there, grind it into dust, and examine that dust through the microscope. It is formed of the decomposed remains of marine animals. So that rock was once at the bottom of the sea. What appalling lapse of centuries has not been necessary to raise so high that which was once buried in the depths of ocean ! Push back indeed, as far as you will, the limits of the world in space and time, yet you do not eliminate God. The creative act still claims recognition. Yet at the first glance it is evident that God appears less than formerly as the *immediate* Cause of all that goes on in the universe. The old form of anthropomorphism is replaced by a new. We no longer imagine the Creator under the image of a workman, the sovereign master of that which He has fashioned.

The imagination tends rather to conceive of Him as of the great magnetic currents which bathe, penetrate, and stir all that exists. His action is no longer that of an all-powerful hand felt though invisible at each moment. It mingles with the play of inexorable laws. The great principle of modern physics, that the sum of energy and the quantity of matter are constant, admits of no derogation. Astronomy establishes it almost experimentally when it shows us that worlds make, unmake, and remake themselves without a single new force or molecule coming into play. Everything is formed slowly, insensibly, with no apparent intervention from without. The very forms of life appear successively throughout periods of infinite length, and the theory which seems to impose itself upon our acceptance is that these forms issue one from the other. It is the same with the history of humanity. There nothing takes place suddenly. Everything is linked together in a chain of growth as in the history of nature. Civilizations are superimposed upon each other like the layers of the palæontological series, and their points of contact are not more clearly marked. Thus determinism is everywhere in evidence, and every day science reduces the number of exceptions. In other words, the modern man eliminates the supernatural from a host of explanations in which the man of the Middle Age thought it was impossible to do without it."

Here is a statement of the origin of the modern theological problem as forcible and clear as R. H. Hutton would have made it. And this author does not for a moment shirk the task of facing it. He sees that the

question of the moment is this : " How far has this
change influenced the religious conceptions of the
European nations ? How far is it necessary to show
favour to this influence in the bosom of Catholicism ? "
I cannot do better than again quote his words, more
especially as they are evidence from within of the attitude
of Liberal Catholics upon the great question of the
inspiration and authority of the Bible. " It is by no
means doubtful that a profound change is being wrought
in Catholic theology. It is only necessary to open a
review to convince one's self of the fact. Though this
change may have more or less distant origins, though it
may be traced back to Dom Calmet or even to Cajetan,
it is none the less true that priests hardly yet forty years
old, trained in the seminaries by masters who are still
living, and with the aid of books which are reprinted
every year, reveal the liveliest surprise when they hear
of a new treatment of Apologetics and of Holy Scripture,
of the superior importance given to the moral proof in
comparison with miracles and prophecy, of profound
modifications in the Introductions to the books of the
Old and the New Testaments, of the discussion of their
historic parts in the same way as the similar writings of
profane authors, of changes in their dates and suspicions
thrown upon their authorship, of ancient difficulties in
their most discussed passages resolved by methods which
are quite new, or rather admitted as if they explained
themselves and exegesis had no need to trouble about
them, of the ' theology ' of the different books studied
separately with a marked freedom, of the study and
examination of the development of these ' theologies,' of

histories of the doctrine of an only God, of that of the angels, of demons, of hell, of the immortality of the soul, of the Holy Spirit, revealing in each case the beginnings, the gropings, the transformations through which they assumed their ultimate form. In what, say these priests, does this method differ from that of sheer rationalism, and above all, how is it to be harmonized with the tradition and teaching of the Councils ? Yet we see that the principles of this school are daily gaining ground, and that with reserves they are securing the support of men of gravity and learning, of trusted members of religious Orders, of publications known for their prudence and orthodoxy." And the conclusion of this author I must again give in his own words. " The Church is allowing herself to be penetrated by the scientific spirit which has been developing by her side during the past three centuries, and evidently believes that in admitting this influence she is caring for her own interests."

But one question inevitably arises. In what way do these Liberals conceive of authority ? What room can they find in their system for an infallible Pope ? Let me quote once again and finally from the author I have followed so long. He is replying to the taunts of those who assert that the Church never makes a step forward until she has been compelled to do so. He claims that such objections arise from a misunderstanding of what the Church is. The Church, for instance, contains a great number of simple, straightforward spirits who have no animosity against science or progress. These people have the very best right to represent the spirit of the Church to which they belong. But perhaps the objectors

have in their mind the central power, the Popes and the
Roman Congregations. Well, authority is before everything else a counterpoise. " Since when has it become
its duty to take the initiative in changes which every
tradition has in the long run to endure ? Where is there
an instance of such a thing ? Authority does not keep
a bureau of science, and, even if it did, it would always
be reproached with being behindhand if it did not anti-
cipate the initiative of genius. Rome is slow, granted.
But it is a less defect than to be fickle and hasty, and for
a responsible authority it is a necessity. It is enough if
she does not fetter the prudent search for truth."

To me the interest of these opinions is the evidence
they yield that the thoughtful men of all the Christian
Communions of Europe are practically at the same point
of view. Whether on the nature of Church authority,
of the inspiration of Scripture, or of the general religious
problem, I can see no appreciable difference between the
positions of M. Dimnet, Professor at the École Jeanne
d'Arc at Lille, and those of the German and Scotch
theologians to whom these French Liberals continually
acknowledge their indebtedness. Only it is a little
amusing to compare the naturalist interpretation of an
infallible authority which holds among Liberal Catholics
of the Roman Communion with the comforting dream
of intellectual passivity and submission in a spiritual
lotus-land which haunts the imagination of those whom
M. Dimnet calls, with I think unnecessary contempt,
" *quelques anglicans très pieux et assez ignorants.*"

CHAPTER III

FRANCE AND THE "AFFAIRE LOISY"

M. LOISY has suddenly—and how much against his will all who know anything of his character and career will readily conceive—been accorded a niche in the temple of newspaper fame—that paradise of the vain and foolish, inferno of wise and humble souls. He has, indeed, had this unhappy greatness thrust upon him, and the hand of destiny is that of the Cardinal Archbishop of Paris. Such English readers as concern themselves with theological wrangles have already had many opportunities of learning something of his case. But it may be worth while to re-state it here, and to attempt to estimate its importance.

March, 1903

First of all let us see what has actually happened. Towards the close of last year M. Loisy published a reply to Harnack's "Das Wesen des Christenthums," entitled "L'Évangile et l'Église." On January 17th of this year, Cardinal Richard, having received the report of a commission which he had appointed to examine Loisy's book, condemned it, and forbade the clergy and faithful of his diocese to read it on the following grounds : "It is calculated seriously to disturb the belief of the faithful in the fundamental dogmas of Catholic teaching, notably the authority of the Scriptures and Tradition, the Divinity of Jesus Christ, His infallible knowledge, the redemption wrought by His death, the Resurrection, the Eucharist, the Divine institution of the Episcopate and of the Sovereign Pontificate." This trenchant condemnation was no doubt not entirely due to the alleged danger of M. Loisy's teaching. A host of other causes concurred to inspire terror in the appointed guardians of scholastic orthodoxy. Early last year the Abbé Houtin, a disciple of Loisy's, had published an account of Biblical criticism among the Catholics of France during the nineteenth century, in which the stupidity of the extreme orthodox champions and the intellectual insincerity of the more moderate were exposed with a corrosive irony. Naturally enough this book became the target for innumerable attacks in which orthodoxy atoned for feebleness of argument by virulence of abuse. For all reply M. Houtin, when a new edition was called for towards the end of the year, published as a supplement to his volume a representative selection of these elegances of controversy. This contemptuous attitude was more than human nature could be expected to bear, and M. Houtin was duly denounced to the Congregation of the Index. Meanwhile the young bloods of the critical movement were laying rude hands on the Sacred Ark. The Abbé Grosjean, a priest of the Diocese of Autun, published in the Abbé Dabry's *Observateur Français* (a Christian Socialist journal, whose title suggests a daring comparison—I know not whether intended—with the official organ of the Vatican) a witty and somewhat irreverent review of Houtin's book. And it was not only in the field of Biblical criticism that scholastic orthodoxy was being assailed. The Abbé Marcel Hébert contributed to the July number of the *Revue de*

Métaphysique et de Morale a study on Divine Personality which he entitled : "La Dernière Idole." The aim of this study, which consisted of a radical and destructive criticism of St. Thomas's proofs of the existence of God, was to prove that "the ancient belief in the transcendent God must yield to the affirmation of the immanent Divine." Strangely enough this audacious defiance of scholasticism is said to have been saved from condemnation by the Spanish Capuchin, Cardinal Vives y Tuto. Still other works are spoken of as likely to be denounced to the Index, among them a study of the theology of Jesus by the Dominican Père Rose, a professor at the Catholic University at Fribourg, in Switzerland. Under this repeated provocation, it is not, perhaps, wonderful if orthodoxy became restive, and determined, when the opportunity was given it, to strike at Loisy regarded as the head and front of this various offending.

The next question which it concerns us to answer, if we would understand the present situation in the Church of France is—who is Loisy ? What kind of man hides behind this name suddenly grown so familiar ? The first impression which anyone who knows his writings will take away is that of a soul tempered to a profound and serene religious faith ; the second, that he has gained that faith and will keep it in obedience to the Roman Church. Perhaps never has the soul of Catholic worship, its universal fitness to human need, been more adequately suggested—and suggestion is here so much more what is needed than dogmatic exposition—than in the last chapter of "L'Évangile et l'Église." But a man is understood as much by what he does as by what he is

behind all action.   And certainly Loisy cannot be understood apart from the life-work which has at once absorbed
and made him.   The key to Loisy is that he is a scholar
and that he knows what is due to scholarship.   There is
not to be found in his pages a single note of insincerity.
He is indefatigable in his pursuit of facts, and absolutely
conscientious in their interpretation.   He seems never
to succumb to that unconscious prejudice which is the
peculiar temptation of the scholar who has a cause to
defend.   Or rather he seems to be the one scholar in a
thousand who has mastered it so completely that it has
vanished without leaving a trace behind, or who has had
the good luck to be free from it from the beginning.
As a very young man, in the early Eighties, Loisy was
appointed Professor of Sacred Scripture at the Catholic
Institute of Paris.   It was the time when some of the
younger and abler seminarists were beginning to feel
out towards a more vital apologetic than that which
they had learned from their traditional handbooks.   In
Paris such men were drawn to the lectures of the École
des Hautes Études, where, under the influence especially
of Auguste Sabatier, they learned to respect and cultivate
a curiosity for the Biblical scholarship of Germany.   Of
these men Loisy was by far the most brilliant, and as
Mgr. d'Hulst, the then leader of the Liberals, reigned
over the Catholic Institute, he was free from vexatious
interference.   But about the beginning of 1893 the
storm which was to hurl Loisy from his chair began to
brew.   Renan had died in the October of 1892.   In the
following January an appreciative article on the great
scholar, written by Mgr. d'Hulst, brought odium not

only upon the Rector of the Catholic Institute, but also upon all who were known to be tarred with the Liberal brush. Besides, in November, Loisy had chosen for the subject of his opening Sessional address at the Institute—"The Biblical question and the inspiration of Scripture." The principle for which he contended in that lecture, which resumed his conclusions from ten years' Biblical study, may be given in a sentence : "All the historical books of Scripture, even those of the New Testament, were formed (*rédigés*) by freer processes than those admitted in the writing of history nowadays, and a certain liberty of interpretation is the legitimate consequence of the liberty which reigns in their composition." This lecture was published in the Spring of 1893, and immediately a fierce agitation against its doctrines began to rage. Loisy was practically forced into the resignation of his chair, and in the Autumn the rout of the Liberals was completed by the publication of the Papal Encyclical *Providentissimus Deus*. Loisy and Mgr. d'Hulst hastened to make dutiful submission to the directions of the Holy Father. The former continued for a time to teach Hebrew and Syriac at the Catholic Institute, but he lived henceforward under the frown of the Diocesan administration. At Bellevue, between Sévres and Meudon, and within easy reach of Paris, he quietly pursued his studies undeterred by poverty and inveterate ill-health. Some years ago the Government nominated him to a lectureship at the École des Hautes Études, where he has drawn large audiences of a class not usually represented in the lecture-room of a religious apologist—many of them students of the École Normale,

in whose hands lie the intellectual destinies of the next
generation of Frenchmen. There he delivered his famous
lectures on the Babylonian myths and the first chapter of
Genesis. Last year he published a remarkable series of
studies on the Gospels—one on the synoptic Parables,
inspired by the recent work of Jülicher of Marburg, the
others on the Gospel of St. John. Then came his reply
to Harnack, and its condemnation by Cardinal Richard,
to which, with ready obedience, he has made the usual
formal submission. The *Semaine Religieuse* of the
diocese of Paris published, in its number of February 7th,
Loisy's letter, in which he stated that he had stopped the
publication of the second edition of his book which was
just on the point of appearing, that he yielded before the
judgment which had been passed, and reproved all the
errors which might have been deduced from his book.
Meanwhile his case goes to Rome, where it is said it
will be tried not before the Congregation of the Index,
but by the newly appointed Biblical Commission.

Two questions remain. What is the nature of Loisy's
teaching ? And what effect is it likely to have on the
Catholicism of France ? The first of these questions it
is not easy to answer adequately in a single paragraph.
But it may be sufficient to say that Loisy's view of dogma
is profoundly different from that of the ordinary Scholastic
apologist. For the latter dogma is practically the object of
faith, the revelation of absolute truth. For Loisy it is
merely the guiding line of religious thought, an aid to
faith. The historical analysis of doctrine reveals the
process of its growth and the factors which have determined its growth. As that historical analysis proceeds,

or rather recedes, we get nearer and nearer to the facts out
of which the Christian life and the Christian doctrine alike
have grown. But we never reach the naked facts themselves. The earliest tradition we possess in which they
are enshrined, the four Gospels, is already a living synthesis of interpretation and fact, a refraction of fact through
the lens of a special interpretation. This is especially the
case for the Gospel of St. John. But even in the Synoptics
this process of interpretation by the early Christian consciousness is apparent. The work of historical criticism is
to reach the actual facts through the first growth of interpretation so far as that is possible. As a critic, Loisy is led
to the most radical results. He will have none of Harnack's
arbitrary separation of our Lord's teaching into the absolute and the relative, that which was eternally true and
that which was conditioned by the knowledge of the time.
For him it was all true, but it was all true because it was
all relative, because it was conditioned throughout by the
knowledge of a given place and time. Nothing is true but
what is true for actual men, and actual men can apprehend
no truth otherwise than through an intellectual medium
determined by their actual experience. Nothing can be
more illusory than the separation of the absolute and the
relative in a living faith. In thought they are separable,
and it is the function of thought to separate them. In
life they are inseparable, and religion is a life. Nor
again will he have any truck with the doctrine that our
Lord consciously accommodated His teaching to the
intellectual disabilities of men. "Jesus spoke," says
Loisy, "in order to say what He thought true, without
the least regard to our categories of relative and absolute."

But it is not necessary that Jesus should have spoken some eternal truth, some truth which in the form he delivered it would have an eternal value. "For the full life of the Gospel does not reside in a single element of the teaching of Jesus, but in the totality of His manifestation which has its point of departure in the personal ministry of the Christ and its development in the history of Christianity. What is truly evangelical in the Christianity of to-day, is not what has never changed, for in one sense everything has changed and has never ceased changing, but that which, notwithstanding all external changes, proceeds from the impulse given by the Christ, is inspired by His spirit, serves the same ideal and the same hope." This is a mere suggestion, but I think not an unfaithful one, of Loisy's position.

As to the influence he is likely to exercise upon the fortunes of French Catholicism, and indeed, of Catholicism generally, it is difficult to strike its balance. There is no doubt, however, that Loisy is followed with an enthusiasm which must often be embarrassing because so heady and undisciplined, by the more intellectual of the younger clergy. The men of the *Justice Sociale* and the men of the *Sillon* are young, and they are, perhaps, not always wise. But at least they have a faith and the consciousness of a mission—two things which carry men a long way. Then, too, there are saner and stronger minds among the younger clergy equally ready to range themselves with the revered master to whose teaching at the Catholic Institute in the early Nineties they look back with gratitude for a faith which can look the best contemporary thought in the face without shame. And even among the more conservative scholars, with a certain reputation for orthodoxy to maintain, Loisy has many open followers, and still more who shrink from declaring themselves, or who, though they are hurrying along the same critical and historical lines, honestly hesitate to touch the goal which he has reached. One can understand the hesitation of an honest scholar like Mgr. Batiffol to accept such extreme conclusions as Loisy's, and his honest regret in having to separate himself from his friend in the moment of trial. On the other hand, that fine scholar and liberal Jesuit, Père de Grandmaison, has written in the Jesuit *Études* an exceedingly appreciative study of Loisy's book. He does not, indeed, accept Loisy's position in full, but at least he shows that he understands it. " It is the book," he says, " of a man who knows the New Testament thoroughly, and the immense literature, especially Protestant, inspired by the Gospels." But it is not by the amount of adhesion to his own special conclusions that Loisy's influence is to be judged. It is by the very general change in the attitude of scholarship towards Biblical and doctrinal questions. Dogmatic theology, the theology of mere definition, has still, indeed, many champions ; among them the well-known Abbé Gayraud, as militant in the pages of the *Revue du Clergé Français* as in the Chamber of Deputies. But historical or positive theology is gaining ground daily among the really scholarly men. Such studies as Mgr. Batiffol's on the origin of the episcopate or of the doctrine of penitence, or M. Turmel's on the early Christian doctrine of the future life, are models of temperate reasoning and honest research. Then, too, there are the Jesuit Biblical scholars, Père Durand and Père de Hummelauer, who are moderate enough, but whose moderation no doubt seems the wildest excess to Père Fontaine, of the same Order, whose scent for Protestant heresy is so keen. Altogether it seems impossible to believe that any power can really crush a movement so virile, so honest, so convinced, and above all so loyal, as the present Liberal movement in the Church of France. It has many powerful and bitter enemies. It has a few ardent friends even in the Curia. But its best friend is its own strength and patience, its inherent conviction and earnestness.

CHAPTER IV

THE INFLUENCE OF LEO XIII

THE long life has come to an end. The greatest figure August, 1903
of the time has vanished from the world of appearances.
We who cannot see beyond our noses begin, as is our
custom, to assess its worth, to appraise its meaning. But
our work, necessary or supererogatory, will be hampered
not alone by our incompetence, but also by the strange
glamour of the mighty soul. Just judgment of the mere
outward effect of the marvellous life must be confused
by the miracle of its inner worth—refracted, as all miraculous things always are, through the lens of popular feeling.
Already the mythoplastic tendency, as they pompously
term it, is at work. M. Galtier, the Rome correspondent
of the *Temps* newspaper, tells us how he learned from
one of the Pope's nephews that all the dying utterances
attributed to the Pope were entirely mythical, that he
had kept a great silence, and almost from the beginning
of his illness had refused to see anyone except his doctors
and the faithful Pio Centra, that even the famous poem
textually quoted (with apologies for the imperfect Latinity
of the telegraph) by all the newspapers was but a product
of the excited imagination of Roman journalism. One
wonders if some acute access of telepathy during this
seething fortnight in Rome can have quite guilelessly
produced such a wonderful result. At least it is clear
that the newspaper and the electric wire have not lessened

the need of surcharged human feeling to express itself worthily in myth.

It is rash, it may be presumptuous, to attempt an estimate of the influence of Leo XIII upon the intellectual life of the great Latin communion. If I do so, it is only from the knowledge that an interested and observant outsider may have. Beyond this I can only plead in explanation or extenuation of my attempt a supreme reverence for the great historical Communion of Western Christendom, a hope that it may prove itself capable of a practical hegemony of the Christianity of the future, and a certainty that it can do so only through its power to absorb and make part of its universal spirit certain elements which are now struggling for effective existence within its pale. From this point of view the interest of Leo XIII is his influence upon the movement towards a more liberal theology which has marked especially the last ten years of his pontificate.

There are here two things to be considered. What is this movement? And what is the scope of any action which authority may have taken with regard to it? After dealing with these points it will be easier to discuss the effects of the last pontificate upon Catholic thought. The quarter of a century during which Leo XIII ruled at the Vatican saw the end of one era and the beginning of another. The critical movement of the middle of the last century, which had originated for the most part either outside historic Christianity or on its extreme fringes, and had developed principally within the narrow paddock of academic Protestantism, was beginning to produce its effect even within the borders of the Roman

Church. It is perhaps natural that the first effect of this movement upon those minds which gradually became aware of its magnitude and import was a tendency to intellectual despair. The close rationalism of the schools —a rationalism, be it understood, traditionally enlisted in the service of faith—served to increase and intensify this despair. Some perhaps submitted to it, trying to get on as best they could with a kind of loose Renanism. But most hardened themselves against it in a more rigid scholastic dogmatism. There are many theologians to-day in the Roman Communion, as in every Christian Communion, who spend their energies in taking away with one hand what they concede with the other—men, for instance, who accept many of the most assured truths of Biblical criticism only to wriggle out of the conclusions to which they point by a tortuous logical process. But, meanwhile, an entirely new school was forming. The object of this school was to get back to a vital certainty of the faith, its inspiration the conviction that that was possible. It has worked along two lines which yet merge into one, a broadened mysticism and a new philosophic defence. The new apologetic, as it is called, is indeed but a reasoned statement of the experiences to which mysticism witnesses. It establishes a reconciliation between philosophy and religion by claiming that the only satisfying answer to the supreme problem of philosophy is given in religious experience. The quest of philosophy is after reality, the thing in itself. Now the thing in itself, pure being, cannot be reached either by the senses or by thought. All that is given in the senses is states of feeling. All that is given in thought is abstractions from these states of feeling. We are always brought up against objects of sensation, objects of thought. But what we seek to know is subjects which feel and know. We want to reach to the absolute of being in ourselves, in other creatures, in God. How, then, is this to be achieved? If, because our sensations or our thoughts do not enable us to reach reality, we were therefore to reject them as illusions, the problem would be insoluble. Scepticism would be the only intelligible outcome of such a view. But thought and feeling are of value, not because they can ever overstep the limits of the phenomenal without us, but because they are expressions, however imperfect and fragmentary, of the real within us. Their value is proportional to our own moral value. They are worth just what we are worth. And our worth is the worth of the total moral will which finds expression in us and through us. It is this total activity of the will which constitutes reality in ourselves, which feels towards and helps reality to constitute itself in others, and which finally reaches beyond the whole sphere of the phenomenal to the absolute being who is God. This is the doctrine of Kant, in so far as that philosopher insists that pure being can only be reached by an affirmation of the moral will. Where it separates from him is in the necessary opposition which he establishes between phenomena and pure being. The real is not apart from and opposed to the appearance. It is in it. It constitutes it. The act of the righteous will which we call faith, and by which we lay hold upon God, is not an act apart from God, but most really in God. That act is possible only because God is in us as the

principle of life.   Yet it is our act, inasmuch as in it we
are consciously making God the end of our activity, and
by doing so are, as it were, helping God to constitute
Himself in ourselves.   It is this double relation of God
to us—as the original principle by which we live and
strive at all, and as the final end towards which all true
life in us is striving—which will resolve most of the
contradictions of Christian thought.   It is the living
reconciliation of immanent and transcendent conceptions
of God, of Pelagian free-will and a determinist view of
Divine grace.

One other point remains to be noted, another antinomy
to be faced, and, if possible, resolved.   If certainty of
reality, if the knowledge of God, is attained from within,
by the harmonious activity of the inner life, in what
relation does this certainty of each stand to that
attained by others and to absolute truth ?   For, even if
it be a certainty of the absolute, it is not in itself an
absolute certainty.   On the contrary, it is imperfect
with the varying degrees of moral imperfection of the
subject which knows.   And it will find still more imperfect expression in intellectual forms.   The truth,
then, does not necessarily correspond to the intellectual
assertion of the certainty of even the holiest life.   Truth—
as much of it as we can have—is rather attained in the
vital reconciliation of all such certainties, in the fusion
which grows out of their living conflict.   Its authority
lies in its necessity as a point of departure for new
experience, as a seed which is sown to fructify in each new
life.   But the mind that receives it is not constrained
by it, is rather liberated by it into the responsibility of

sounding more adequately the hidden depths of life. Truth is a growing thing, because life is a growing thing —" no end to growth." It lies in the values which the life of love, the life of that self which has attained oneness with the not-self, affirms as its most positive certainties.

This is something like the philosophic attitude of the New Apologetic. In this form it has found expression through a few profound and original minds—some of them laymen. But the spirit which animates it, the positive spirit, the spirit which trusts life as a revelation of God, is at work in many other directions. It is transforming the old asceticism, giving it a more positive content, making it selective and intensive, rather than merely negative, in its dealings with life. Through the life of Father Hecker it is reaching out with promise of profound modification for the Catholicism of America. The leaven of the Paulist Fathers in New York, for instance, is working vigorously in the lump. But what is the attitude of authority towards this movement, and what can authority effect ? Let me take the last question first. Authority can effect nothing against it, for two reasons. First, it is profoundly Catholic. It has the living tradition of Catholicism in its favour. It is opposed only by and to the dead hand of recent scholastic orthodoxy. At the Reformation the Catholicism of the Roman Communion was cooped in behind fenced walls. There it has ever since remained, strictly on the defensive, using every weapon of the scholastic armoury to repel attack. Now the field is once more clear for the recovery and the development of a vital theology. The attack

of Protestantism has died away into an impotent mimicry
of warfare among its less instructed zealots. The old
guard of Catholicism does not yet realize this. But the
new men will some day persuade, by the mere tenacity
and force of their conviction, even them. Then the day
for restoring and broadening the living tradition of
Catholic theology in terms of current thinking will have
arrived. And, secondly, the function of authority is
itself being gradually modified, both in practice and in
theory. The responsibility of infallibility, in a world
where the most sacred utterances are so easily convicted
of some degree of fallibility, is simply too great a risk.
And so the meaning of the word is being gradually
whittled away. A recent Roman writer has told us that
the conditions of infallibility as laid down in the Vatican
decree have obtained only in two decisions during the
whole course of the Church's history, possibly only in
one. And it is not impossible that an ingenious dialectic
might discover even that one to be uncertain. But
what is still more probable is that the conditions of the
Vatican decree will never be met in any future pronouncement of authority. Meanwhile a new positive
view of authority is shaping itself as an integral part of
that philosophy of will and liberty which I have outlined
above. In that authority the *Ecclesia discens*—the
garnered experience of all holy souls, the free and unfettered analysis of what that experience imports, the
work of the Church's thinkers in kneading the results of
that analysis into the forms of contemporary thought—
will have its part, and that the most important, the
formative, part. The *Magisterium infallibile* will but

reprove the rawness of haste, check the excesses of individualism, and register the final collective result. After all, that is the true function of authority, and it will prevail.

And now, what has been the attitude of Leo XIII, or, rather, of the Roman authority during his pontificate, towards this movement? For an answer to that question is in the main an account of his influence upon the intellectual life of the Roman Church. No one, I think, can help feeling a profound reverence for the vivid intelligence which in an extreme old age was eager to face new problems unfamiliar to the intellectual atmosphere in which it had itself been formed. That is the first feeling one has about this great ecclesiastical ruler in his dealings with things of the intellect. But having expressed it, one is the more free to assert that he had not, and, in the nature of things, could not have had, any real living sympathy with the men of the last two decades of the nineteenth century. His instinct was that of repression, though it was tempered by the wisdom and patience of a really great ruler. There was indeed something of irony in the fact that his own personal enthusiasm for St. Thomas Aquinas led him to make an effort to revive Scholasticism at the very moment when it was being threatened by the inroads of a more modern philosophy. The Encyclical *Æterni Patris* did something, no doubt, to impart a certain vigour and virility to Catholic dialectic. It did nothing to stimulate Catholic thought. The most it did was to give a fillip to the fading energies of the universities of Louvain and Rome, and to prepare a generation of hard controversialists for the coming duel with the new apologists. The next Encyclical on matters theological was the famous *Providentissimus Deus*, issued on November 18th, 1893. This was directly called forth by the acute phase of the Biblical controversy which had then been reached, especially in France. The total effect of that Encyclical was, as it was meant to be, to make it next to impossible for the critics to continue their work. For instance, the internal criticism by which the origin, the authority, and the integrity of every book of Scripture were to be assured, and which a distinguished French bishop had in that very year declared to have obtained " le droit de cité " among all parties, was ruthlessly rejected, except in so far as it might serve to bolster up the historical tradition on those points. But the boldest declaration of this Encyclical, and that which it has been hardest for the critical school ever since to evade, was that on inspiration. " All those books, and those books in their entirety, which the Church regards as sacred and canonical were written with all their parts under the inspiration of the Holy Spirit. Now, far from admitting the co-existence of error, Divine inspiration by itself excludes all error, and that also of necessity, since God, the Supreme Truth, must be incapable of teaching error." It is evident that this view of inspiration tended to make the natural development of Biblical study in the Roman Church extremely difficult. Yet, in spite of the Encyclical, criticism flourishes and numbers among its adepts many who are in all matters of philosophic apology the most unbending of old scholastics. Finally, there was the letter to Cardinal Gibbons, *Testem Benevolentiæ*, in which the obscuration and attenuation of doctrine imputed to Americanism were condemned. In all these ways the authority of the late Pontificate tended to depress and hamper the men who were labouring in the sweat of their souls for the intellectual restoration of the Christian faith, and to encourage and sustain those whose only conception of defence was to insulate the edifice of truth from all touch with the living world. That is a task sufficiently hard of accomplishment. In the words of a great Catholic scholar, " Catholic exegetes cannot make the theology of the past the science of to-day." But it is a misfortune that in their attempt to do so they should have been reinforced by the support of a venerable authority.

CHAPTER V

THE " UNKNOWN POPE "

Two years ago in Vienna I spent a delightful afternoon *September,* of late April in the Prater discussing the coming Conclave 1903 with an Austrian publicist who had for long lived in Rome as representative of the *Neue Freie Presse*, and had there acquired a detailed and accurate knowledge of ecclesiastical affairs.   There were few Cardinals, Papabili or otherwise, who were not passed in review during those two hours' conversation.   But there was one whose name provoked only the most passing and distant allusion— the then Cardinal Patriarch of Venice.   The Conclave, which was then but a certainty of some uncertain future, is now a thing of the past.   Cardinal Sarto has become Pius X, the little-known Venetian Patriarch the " Un- known Pope," as the French, with their *flair* for the right phrase, have already styled him.   So is history made—in great moments of birth, of death, of unalterable choice.

The election of Pius X may be a revolution.   Who knows ?   The great spirit of history may have spoken a word big with fate in the Conclave of July, 1903.   At least in its accidental features this election is the begin- ning of a new era or the reversion to an old.   The Pope is still indeed Italian, but no longer an Italian of the old school, a noble trained in the traditional diplomacy of the Papal Court, graduating in distant nunciatures or legations.   Pius X has never been, like his predecessor,

205

Pontifical Legate at Beneventum, or Nuncio at Brussels. The son of the peasant of Riesi has from the beginning shared the life of the secular priesthood. As parish priest of Salzano, as Bishop of Mantua, as Patriarch of Venice, he has all his life been absorbed in the details of parochial or diocesan administration. In the words of the Paris *Temps*, " Son élection est comme l'apothéose du curé de campagne." But more than that, the new Pope has remained what he was born, a son of the people, simple with their simplicity, alive to their needs, aware of their difficulties, eager for their permanent reconciliation with the Church, above all convinced that the Church must be the Church of the poor if it is to endure. The old democratic days seem to have come again. We recall the far-distant time when the waif of the Cypriote shore, fathered by a kindly fisherman, came to sit for a few perilous months on the Throne of the Fisherman as Alexander V.

But after all these are or may be but mere accidents of the new situation. We have no right to count on them as factors of permanent importance. The policy of the Vatican is run in a groove of too ancient routine to be lightly displaced by a personality, and especially by a personality on which we can so little calculate. The forces of the Roman Curia are forces to which Pius X. may be ready to yield or forced to succumb. And what interests the outside world is whether the election of the new Pope will mean a conflict of opinion at all; and if it does, whether the new forces or the old will win. Alike in affairs of international politics and in matters of belief, a new spirit is making itself felt in the Roman

Church, a new attitude is being urgently called for. Will the new pontificate take account of one or the other; and if it does, will it do justice to them ?

I have already in these chapters dealt with the critical leaven which is working in the Roman Church, as elsewhere throughout Christendom, with the attempt to correct the rigidly dogmatic by the historical point of view. It is difficult to forecast the effect of the New Pontificate upon this movement. But whatever change in the attitude of the Roman Curia towards dogmatic questions may be effected in our time will, we may be sure, be largely if not entirely influenced by political or semi-political considerations. The Curia will not move till America and Germany force it to move, till the spirit of Hecker and of Kraus has become so powerful and insistent as to make further resistance dangerous. It is impossible to avoid the fear that in the near future, as in the past, the Papacy will elect to challenge the judgment of history on its political action. Now there is one country in which the future policy of the Vatican will be awaited with interest, not only within the borders of that country, but by all who, of whatever country, are preoccupied with the future of the Roman Church. I need hardly say that that country is France. Leo XIII was a Pope of considerable political imagination and of vast political schemes. His policy succeeded in many countries, notably in Germany, where it formed in the great Catholic party of the Centre a most formidable political power. But in France it failed utterly. When the late Pope called upon the Catholics of France to rally to the Republic, his object was transparent. He hoped to form a powerful Catholic party which, as in Germany, might hold the balance between the strictly national groups of Liberals and Conservatives, or, as in Belgium, might even itself seize the reins of government. He failed because the French Catholics pointedly refused to obey him. The clergy indeed obeyed under a hardly veiled protest. The laity were more obstinate. Instead of obeying they prayed for his conversion, and appealed in the clerical press from the Pope ill-informed to the Pope better-informed. Not only did the obstinacy of the pious laity wreck the policy, at once generous and shrewd, of Leo XIII, but it also wantonly aggravated its own hostility towards the Republic until it had provoked that violent outburst of anti-clericalism from which France is at the present moment suffering. There is an intimate, if also a somewhat intricate relation of cause and effect between the Papal policy of " ralliement " and the intolerant administration of M. Combes. And it is surely a sign of the times worth noting, that the most violent and uncompromising statement of State policy towards the Church which has ever fallen from the lips of a French Premier, the now famous "Marseillaise "* of M. Combes, should have followed by only a few days' interval the election of the new Pope. It means something that after eighteen months of continuous protest from all the Liberals of France, whether official or non-official, against his treatment of the Congregations, M. Combes can still venture to proclaim a continuance and even an aggravation of his policy. And it seems to me to mean just this,

* A newspaper title for the Minister's speech, which was delivered at Marseilles.

that the French Catholics are so reactionary as to provoke the most violent policy of persecution among the extreme anti-clerical section of Republicans, and at the same time so powerful as to concentrate at critical moments the Republican Block in support of that policy, detested as it is by many members and even whole groups of the Republican party. M. Combes' ministry may indeed fall in the autumn, and every Liberal would rejoice in its fall but for the possible danger to the Republic. But one thing must not be forgotten, that what makes the *intransigeance* of the present Government possible is the determined and hopeless hostility of French Catholics to the Republic, and their incessant intrigues against it. The political judgments of the foreigner are often influenced by considerations of the attitude of particular individuals which to the native mind seem negligible, or at least unimportant. One such consideration has weighed with me in my observation of French politics during the last few years. It is not many years ago that M. Francis de Pressensé, the brilliant scion of an ancient Huguenot stock, wrote his famous life of Cardinal Manning, and his still more famous Introduction. Many people, and among them M. de Pressensé's own friends, feared that that Introduction was only a preliminary to his joining the Roman Church. Well, to-day M. de Pressensé is one of the foremost of the Socialist deputies in the Chamber, and the author of a drastic " projet de loi " for the separation of Church and State in France. It was the venomous hatred of the Republic displayed by French Catholics during the course of the Dreyfus struggle that wrought that change.

What, then, might a well-wisher at once of Liberalism
and of the French Church hope that the attitude of the
new Pope should be ? There is no doubt about the
answer. The only attitude which can preserve both
Liberalism and the Church is a frank abandonment of
political action. The Church cares little possibly for
the fate of Liberalism, though when the last vestige
of its moderating influence disappears from Catholic
countries, when it has everywhere yielded to a rabid
Jacobinism, she may learn the folly of even that indifference. But at least she ought to care for the interests
of religion. And the fortunes of organized Christianity
will be wrecked throughout Catholic Europe unless the
Church abandons her traditional ideal of asserting herself
as a great political force. A solid political Catholicism
is the nightmare which is driving so many European
States into precipitate and ill-considered action. Even
in Protestant States like Germany it is producing evil,
or at least unnatural, results. Social Democracy is a
growing power in the Fatherland far more from fear of
the Centre than from love of Socialism. And in France
the only hope of Catholicism is in political inactivity
on the part of the Vatican. " In returning and rest
shall ye be saved : in quietness and in confidence shall
be your strength." Leo XIII found even French
Catholicism recalcitrant to his political schemes. It was
natural. The traditions of generations are not to be
reversed in a night. It is not possible for any outside
force, even the strongest, suddenly to regiment whole
masses of men, hereditarily committed to a given policy
with all its far-reaching consequences, in a new direction.

And for French Catholics the political dreams of Leo XIII constituted an outside force. The political change of attitude which must in time declare itself among French Catholics will be of slow and gradual growth. It will be accomplished in individuals, and according to the psychology of the individual, in order that it may be accomplished in the mass. The most politically intelligent will first and almost unconsciously accommodate themselves to the changed conditions, as indeed they have already done and are doing. The politically stupid and unteachable must remain where they are and perhaps for generations. But the dream of forcing united action is both delusive and fatal. It cannot succeed, and its very failure, as the experience of the last ten years has amply shown, only increases the mischief which its success would not have averted. The bugbear of the modern politician, especially in Catholic countries, is the obvious desire of the Church to force herself as a wedge between the parties which represent the natural political development of nations, the parties of inactivity and of progress. The Church as a political force can only be a disturbing element in national development, and the politician is wise in the instinct which regards her as the enemy in so far as she insists on being such. Her mission is of another order and in another sphere. Even in France, if only the evil traditions of a century could be obliterated, the Jacobinism which supports M. Combes or goads him into extreme action would crumble to pieces. He is now supported by thousands who long for the day when Liberalism may regain its humanising sway, and alas! long in vain. And their longing will continue to be vain while the fear of a united Catholic party, either rigidly fixed in its own bitter mood of reaction or rallied by the Pope to the cause of the Republic, troubles the dreams of politicians.

It is not wonderful if the Liberalism of France remembers with relief that the new Pope is not a diplomatist, but a mere ecclesiastic, and hopes against hope that he may continue to be an ecclesiastic and refuse the temptation to become a politician. It is a little inconsequent of them—but human nature, and especially political human nature, being what it is, perhaps also natural— to be jubilant over the rumour that he belongs to the French or Rampollist party at the Vatican rather than to the Vannutellist or Austrian. At any rate the religious future of Catholicism, in other words of organized Christianity, depends upon the political neutralization of the Vatican. The " Unknown Pope " may be able and willing to reverse tradition. It is a feeble hope, but it is a hope worth cherishing. Meanwhile *on espère et on verra !*

CHAPTER VI

THE FIRST ENCYCLICAL OF PIUS X

In the September number of the *Commonwealth*, when the new Pope was still an unknown force, I expressed the hope that the election of Pius X might be the beginning of a new era at the Vatican ; that the entail of Curial diplomacy might at last be broken ; that the Church, through its responsible head, might for the future devote itself only to the spiritual guidance of Christendom, and abandon the fantastic heritage of merely Italian politics bequeathed to it by the dead hand of past history. The hope, I admitted, was a feeble one. It is all the more necessary to recognize the signs of a more ample and immediate fulfilment of it than could have been expected. The relations which Pius X has already established with the clergy and people of Rome are those of a true spiritual pastor. It is delightful to read of those Sunday afternoon gatherings in the Vatican gardens, when the people of the different Roman " regions " assemble to hear from the lips of their Chief Pastor the simple words of the Eternal Gospel. It is equally delightful to hear that the Bishop of Rome, like any simple diocesan bishop, calls his clergy together to receive his guidance and encouragement in the discharge of their spiritual duties. It is facts like these that justify the prediction of a recent writer in the *Quinzaine*, one who knew Pius X intimately before his elevation to the Pontificate : " He will talk less than Leo XIII, but perhaps he will do more."

December, 1903

There is hope, too, that what seems to an outsider the grotesque anachronism of the Captivity may soon come to an end, and that the Roman crowd may yet acclaim the passing of the Pope, no longer King, in the Corso or the Via Nazionale.

But to me the most significant change in the aim and direction of Papal policy is indicated in the tone of the encyclical letter of October 4th. · There are, as we shall see, disquieting aspects about that letter. Yet it must be admitted that the aspects to which I refer would prove disquieting to but a very small proportion of the members of the Roman Communion, and to a still small, if somewhat larger, proportion of Christians outside the Roman pale. To the great majority they would count, no doubt, as most reassuring. In any case I have no desire to touch upon them just now. My immediate purpose is to call attention to the spiritual earnestness and purpose which pervade this letter, and to the almost entire absence from it of political implications. Even the temporal power is only distantly hinted at in a single passing phrase, and that, perhaps, the most conventional and least convincing in the whole letter. On the other hand, though every sentence taken by itself may be commonplace in conception and conventional in expression, there glows throughout the whole a spiritual ardour which reveals the directness and simplicity of a personal, as distinguished from a merely official, ideal of duty.

Already the spirit of Pius X is being reflected in France. The most significant episcopal pronouncement of recent times is the pastoral letter which Mgr. Fuzet,

Archbishop of Rouen, has just issued to his clergy. Taken with an article written earlier in the year by M. Birot, the Vicar General of Mgr. Mignot's diocese of Albi, and almost certainly representing the views of the Archbishop of Albi himself, it points to a change of policy on the part of French Catholics which, if not too late, may be full of fruitful and happy consequence for the future of the Church in France. It is a matter of common knowledge that the same policy is strenuously advocated by Mgr. Lacroix, Bishop of Tarentaise. Mgr. Fuzet could not be more explicit. He calls upon his clergy to hold themselves aloof from the tumultuous arena agitated by political passions ; to avoid the " commotions of a bitter, irascible, unforgiving zeal," to refrain from taking part in " political conferences, banquets, or processions organized by our associations." " If we wish," he continues, " to hold France for the Church, it is high time to return to that patient charity which is not easily provoked, which beareth all things, and which knows how to raise itself above secondary questions in which first principles are not involved. To secure religious peace, let us refuse no accommodation which leaves the faith untouched." These words, uttered at a time when the Concordat is endangered, when the repeal of the Loi Falloux, in so far as it guaranteed to the authorized Orders and the secular clergy the right of teaching, is on the eve of being accomplished, when the Orders themselves have to face wholesale suppression, and often in circumstances (generally, it must be admitted, of their own creation) of legal indignity,—may seem a cowardly shirking of a great issue.

To me they seem, on the contrary, the words of wisdom
and moderation, inspired by a just view of the political
situation. It is unnecessary to say that they have been
met by a storm of abuse, alike from the extreme Clericals
who hate the Republic, and from the extreme Radicals
who hate the Church. Mgr. Fuzet is for the moment
the common target for the grossest missiles of scorn
which the ingenuity of extreme sectaries can devise.
The Radicals, of course, accuse him of having his eye on
the vacancy in the Archbishopric of Paris, which the
death of the aged and infirm Cardinal Richard may
any day create. To the extreme Clericals he is simply a
traitor. The reactionary Bishops, with the fiery Mgr.
Turinaz at their head, have promptly fulminated in a
contrary sense. None the less, Mgr. Fuzet and those
who act with him are the one hope of the Church at a
moment of supreme crisis. The Republican Block,
dominated by M. Jaurès, and by even fiercer spirits than
he, holds the occasionally hesitant M. Combes in the hollow
of its hand. The Jacobin spirit is triumphant. Passive
obedience to the dictates of the Block has become the
one political virtue. The ideal of Ignatius Loyola, to
become like a corpse in the hands of authority, is the
ideal which Jacobin fanaticism is prepared to impose
upon every minister, as well as upon every member of the
majority in the Chamber. M. Lintilhac parades his
autocratic tags from Aristotle in the Senate with an
effrontery which would not have been unworthy of
Napoleon himself. It seems as if the liberties of the
Catholic minority were to be completely suppressed.
And yet all this is possible only because of the political

intransigeance of the Clericals—an *intransigeance* at once stupid and unteachable. And it will continue to be possible so long as that spirit continues. That is just what the few intelligent Churchmen in France so clearly see. M. Fonsegrive (known perhaps best to English readers under his pseudonym of Yves le Querdec), has recently stated in the *Quinzaine* that he and other Catholic Liberals have probably conceded too much in the past to the prejudices of the extreme wing, that they ought all along to have fought more boldly and openly for the idea of Liberalism in Catholic politics. M. Fonsegrive is quite right. It is the hour for compromise, for a frank acceptance of the Republic by Catholics, for political action on the part of Catholic laymen in concert with the Progressist Liberal party. That party is reconstituting itself. The cause of Liberalism for which it stands is daily championed in the Press by the foremost minds of France, often by men who could not identify themselves politically with M. Méline. M. Clemenceau has just urged in the Senate one of the most powerful pleas for liberty which have been heard there for years. Perhaps a still more significant fact is the speech of M. Charles Dupuy, formerly President of the Council, delivered in the Senate on November 5th. For in that speech he buttressed his appeal for liberty of teaching by a reference to the changed tone of Catholic theology, to its openness to the influence of modern knowledge and modern habits of thought, as indicated by M. Loisy's " L'Évangile et L'Église "—a name which, as M. Dupuy added, was on all men's lips. It is certainly not usual for an ex-Radical Minister to defend his political action by a reference to the writings of a Catholic divine, just as it is unusual to find such writings available for such a purpose. The forces of Liberalism would not only be enormously strengthened, they would be speedily triumphant, if only the policy advocated by Mgr. Fuzet could be frankly accepted by even a respectable minority of the Catholics of France. It would mean, of course, the abandonment for the moment of the cause of the Congregations, but it would mean also the preservation of the Concordat, which without such a change of policy seems inevitably doomed. It is of course but a feeble hope that such prudent counsels will prevail. But at least the temper of the new Encyclical is a direct encouragement to those who may be courageous enough to adopt and follow them.

The influence of the Church in the future must depend upon her spiritual methods and aims, no longer upon mere political chicanery. Every attempt to extend her mere political influence is a direct loss of effective power. It is on this account that we may hope that the dream of installing a Papal Nuncio at the court of St. James's, which it is said is again haunting the brains of certain ecclesiastics both in England and in Rome, will come to nothing. There is, indeed, in any case little chance of its success. The temper of England is touchy and irritable at the mere suggestion of such schemes. The instinct which will resist them may be largely the product of ignorance and prejudice, but in the main it is a right instinct. No religion will make its way in the future but in virtue of its own inherent worthiness, of its correspondence to the actual needs of humanity. If the

Catholicism of the Roman Church is to make its way, it must not attempt to exempt itself from the conditions of success which are being everywhere set by the trend of the modern spirit. Among these none is more certain than a view of religion which, however much it may allow for the claims of organization and the need of authority, yet claims for the individual the right to apply it as he will in all the multiform concerns of the secular life. The religion which seeks to regiment its adherents politically is to that extent doomed as a living spiritual force. It must inevitably sink to the level of a semi-political semi-religious sect, about the most grotesque and antiquated absurdity which can still cumber God's earth.

It is on this account that I recognize with satisfaction the new note of the Encyclical *E Supremi Apostolatus*. I wish I could look forward with equal hope to the influence of Pius X upon the future of the heroic attempts which are being made by the young scholars of France and Italy to present the faith in an intellectual form likely to commend itself to modern habits of thought. For any such hope I can only say with regret that I see no support. Pius X is not a theologian. He is almost a saint, with all the narrowness and intensity of a man of meagre intellect and strong conviction. He is all the more dangerous on that account. The new Papal Secretary may have a wider range of intellectual interests, but he is said by those who know him to be a man of the same stamp, sincere, courageous, straightforward, convinced that the faith is coterminous with its traditional interpretation. Those of us who believe that the future of the faith depends in a supreme degree upon the wise application of the results and habits of contemporary thinking to the fresh interpretation of its contents may yet long for one of the days of Rampolla, may live to regret the veto which the Archbishop of Cracow carried in his pocket into the Conclave and which indirectly lifted Cardinal Sarto into the Apostolic Chair.

CHAPTER VII

THE SEPARATION LAW OF 1905

THE Napoleonic agreement with the Supreme Pontiff *August* 1905
has outstayed its welcome while. It has succeeded in
completing its century, insisting besides upon its three
years of grace. With the last day of 1905 it will no
doubt finally cease to be ; for the Luxembourg is not
likely even to modify the decisions of the Palais Bourbon.
For long this strange treaty has clung a dead leaf to the
tree of history. Only a belated blast of a great storm of
popular indignation has at last swept it away. Or can
we say even that ? For rather it seems to have fallen
by chance after the passing of the storm, under the
benediction of the recovered sunshine and amidst the
quiet laughter of peaceful airs. Æolus, in the person of
M. Combes, had retired to his cave, and the calm head
of Neptune Rouvier appeared above the waves. It is a
change of metaphor, but the situation permits and even
demands a good many.

Nothing certainly is more astonishing than the
universal satisfaction amid which this project of separation
has been completed, except perhaps the passion and the
terror with which it was inaugurated. Were they both
a little feigned ? Did the fiercest anti-clerical sincerely
believe that separation would clip the Church's talons,
or the most obstinate Ultramontane fear that it would
clip her wings ? We are at least permitted to doubt it,

now that the result leaves all but the most irreconcilable extremists on either side satisfied. The power of the Church to hurt and destroy in the mountain of Republican politics and to soar in the free air of its native spirit remains exactly what it was before. Perhaps it is a perception of this fact, added to the studied moderation of the Legislature in its references during the discussion of the Bill to members of the dissolved Congregations, that accounts for the favour with which most of these have received a measure whose absolute condemnation at their hands might well have been expected. At any rate the fact remains, that they have for the most part accepted it with something like satisfaction, and it is even said that their influence has been steadily directed to procuring its favourable reception by the Roman Curia.

But if the Bill will leave the legitimate power of the Church intact, and may fail to reduce appreciably its interference in secular politics, nay, may even intensify the danger for the present democratic Republic of that interference, it is none the less a gain that it should be passed. For it creates an honest situation all round. There is always something confusing for the moral sense and disconcerting for the moral judgment in a compact between things so unequal and dissimilar as a spiritual and a temporal power. The least exercise of power on the part of the temporal partner in the compact can be construed into an appearance of tyranny. The most unwarrantable use of spiritual power can save itself from condemnation, and even procure for itself a certain measure of respect, at least with those who do not immediately suffer from it, and they are always the greater number. It has been so conspicuously in the relations between the French State and the Vatican under the Concordat. The situation which that compact created was confused from the beginning, and it remains confused till the end. The Organic Articles, for instance, have never been recognized by the Roman Court. The Concordat was a treaty between the French State and the Curia. The Organic Articles were certain regulations determining the relations of the French Church, regarded as national, and the civil administration. In these no foreign power had the right of interference. Yet it is clear that the Pope was not likely to admit—and with the growth of Ultramontanism was less and less likely to admit—the validity of such internal arrangements between Church and State. But the very act by which the Concordat gained effect on French territory, the law of the 18th Germinal in the year X of the Republic, incorporated the Organic Articles with the treaty. So that from the beginning and in the very constitution of the compact the elements of friction existed. It is not wonderful that a treaty between powers so unequally matched, and vitiated by the inherence of such radical defects, has tried all the skill of diplomatists to work it at all. It is still less wonderful that it has frequently broken down altogether, and that in late years it has resulted in a deadlock which threatened in time to paralyse the Church's action. No one can mistake the significance of twenty vacant bishoprics which disputed interpretations of the Concordat are leaving as a legacy to the new régime.

Granted the necessity of this measure of political honesty and sincerity, it has been carried through with a scrupulous regard for justice and even for traditional religious sentiment which does honour to Republican France. And it is interesting to notice that the man who, as Reporter of this Bill, has displayed the most liberal, intelligent and sympathetic statesmanship, is a socialist—M. Aristide Briand, the still youthful deputy of the Loire. The general form of the Bill is determined by the fact that at present all expenses incident upon the exercise of public worship—Catholic, Protestant and Jewish—are a charge upon the State Budget and upon certain Departmental and Communal Budgets. All such charges are suppressed from the 1st of January of next year. The present ecclesiastical establishments will, however, continue to use and administer all the ecclesiastical property at present under their direction until they have transferred it to the new associations for worship (*associations cultuelles*), which they must do within a year from the date on which the law comes into operation. All Cathedrals, Churches, Chapels, Temples, and Synagogues, which are at present, in accordance with the law of the 18th Germinal in the year X, appropriated by the State to the exercise of public worship, or which have been provided by the State for the same purpose since that date, will continue to be State property, and by it will continue to be appropriated to the ecclesiastical establishments which at present use them, and to their successors the Associations. Archbishops' and Bishops' houses will be in the same way freely placed by the State at the disposition of the present ecclesiastical establishments and the Associations to which they may transfer them, during a period of two years. Presbyteries, the " Grands Séminaires," and the Protestant Theological Faculties will be freely continued in the possession of their present directors and the Associations which will legally succeed them, for a period of five years. At the end of these periods, the further disposition of all these buildings will be resumed by the State, the Departments, or the Communes to which they belong. Where there is no Presbytery and the Commune has provided the rent of the Minister's house, it is still called upon to do so during a period of five years. All buildings are granted on condition that they are kept in sufficient repair by the Association. Certain buildings having an artistic or historical value will be placed in a class by themselves, and no " restoration " may be attempted upon them without the authority of the Minister of Fine Arts, or may be executed without the superintendence of his department. So that Church Vandalism will not in France be a private amusement, but, when it occurs in the future, a national sin.

All ministers of religion who are over 60 and who have been for 30 years performing ecclesiastical duties paid for by the State, will receive an annual pension for life equal to three-fourths of their present salary. Those who are over 45, and have been paid by the State for at least 20 years, will receive a life pension equal to half of their present salary. All others will receive a grant of the whole of their present yearly salary for the first year after the Separation, two-thirds for the second, a half for the third, and a third for the fourth year ; except that in the case of Communes of less than 1,000 inhabitants, and for their present ministers of religion who will continue to serve in them, the duration of each of the above periods will be doubled.

The religious unit recognized by the State will be for the future the " Association for worship " formed in each Commune. In Communes of less than 1,000 inhabitants, seven persons may form such an Association. In Communes of from 1,000 to 20,000 inhabitants, an Association must consist of at least 15 persons, and in Communes of over 20,000 inhabitants, of 25. These Associations must hold a general meeting once a year, to consider and approve the yearly statement of finance. They must receive and control all collections and offerings for the expenses of worship, all payments for religious services and ceremonies, pew-rents (it is the nearest English I can find for " *la location des bancs et sièges* "), etc. They can freely transfer to other Associations formed for a like purpose any surplus of their receipts over expenditure. They must in no form receive subventions from the State, Departments or Communes, except grants made for repairs to buildings under their control which may be classed as public monuments. The Associations can form themselves into Unions with a central administration. Associations and Unions must submit their financial position to the control of the Inspector-General of Finances. For the purpose of assuring the expenses and maintenance of worship, both Associations and Unions can form a reserve fund not exceeding three times their average annual income, if that income is more than 5,000 francs, not exceeding six times their income if it is

less than 5,000 francs.   In addition they can establish a
special reserve for building purposes, or for the decoration
and repair of the fabric and furniture of the Churches or
other buildings entrusted to them.   Finally, all Churches
are exempt from the land tax and from the door and
window tax, while Presbyteries, Seminaries and the
Protestant Faculties of Theology are subject to the same
taxes as the property of private persons.

The provisions of the 5th " Title " of the law, which
deals with " *police des cultes*," have little interest.   They
are largely a repetition of certain provisions of the
Organic Articles.   One of the most interesting (to an
Irishman) is the attachment of certain penalties to the
boycotting of any citizen for attending or refusing to
attend public worship.   But readers of the *Commonwealth* may be more interested to know that religious
instruction may not be given, under a penalty, to children of school age and on the rolls of public schools, save
outside school hours.

Now, as a Churchman, I claim that this Bill is a just
and statesmanlike attempt to disentangle an exceedingly
confused situation, that it fully guarantees individual
liberty of conscience, that it gives the Church perfect
freedom of action within her legitimate sphere, which by
elimination it defines.   It is a clear, practical analysis of
the idea of a Church, or rather of the concrete fact of a
Church as it presents itself to the disinterested State.
The Church's conception of what would be just treatment
for herself at the hands of the State is an utterly fantastic
one, because it proceeds from an unwarranted assumption,
the assumption, viz., that the State takes the same view

of her nature and character which she herself must take in order to be true to herself. But this is not true of the modern State, and if it were true it would, in view of actual religious differences, inevitably lead to injustice. For the practical and impartial State the Church is an Association of Associations. The concrete religious unit is an Association of persons in a certain place formed and continuing to exist for the exercise of a certain form of worship. Religious freedom is the freedom of individuals to form such Associations, and the freedom of such Associations to enter into union with one another on such terms as they may themselves determine. This liberty is, as it seems to me, punctiliously provided for by the French Bill. The Church returns to the pre-Constantinian stage, with the important distinction that the State does not discriminate against it as one of the religious Associations with which it is the duty of the State to deal. The Church in France is for the future free to develop herself as a purely spiritual power and by purely spiritual means. The adventitious help or hindrance of connection with the State is removed. Her work will no longer wear the appearance of being part of the national administration. Its cost will be no longer charged, and that quite insufficiently for real effectiveness, to the national Budget. Her officers will no longer have their temporal dignity unworthily enhanced or their spiritual freedom unworthily compromised by being also State officials. In short, the Church, not being national in fact, will no longer be able to assume the pretence of being national.

What, then, will be the effect of this measure upon the

future of the Church in France ? It is a question on which intelligent French Catholics are themselves much divided. Naturally, the opinion of an outsider is worth little. But at least it may be supposed that there must be grounds for hope when we see such good Catholics and such intelligent and far-seeing minds as M. Fonsegrive and the Comte d'Haussonville ranged on the side of Separation as ardent partisans. The situation at least is clear. There are, perhaps, to make the most liberal computation, 8,000,000 practising Catholics in France— about a fifth of its total population. The question of finance will probably not be troublesome. As for the personnel of the hierarchy, it will no doubt undergo an immediate and a radical transformation. The Vatican will be able to nominate on the morrow of Separation to a fourth of the total number of dioceses in France. Besides, many, one might say most, of the present occupants of sees are old men. In a few years the fortunes of the French Church, in so far as they can be determined by the character of its officers, will depend upon the unfettered choice of Rome. There is little doubt that the vacant Bishoprics, and others as they become vacant, will be filled by members of the dissolved Congregations. The chief difficulty will lie in obtaining officers of the lower rank for the spiritual army. The French peasant, and it is from the peasantry that these officers have in the past been drawn, is a natural admirer of official rank. It appeals both to his economic and his æsthetic instincts. He covets its security and its dignity. There will almost certainly be a considerable falling off in the supply of candidates for the priesthood, and that, without unduly impugning the motives which lead men in France, as elsewhere, to offer themselves for service in the Church. Besides, it must be remembered that in France, at any rate, the choice of the ministry does not rest with the future priest himself, but with the quite natural and legitimate ambition of parents. His career is already determined by the time he has reached the age of thirteen. As a rule his vocation is fixed on the day that he enters the " *petit séminaire.*" But the greatest danger which the free Church has to face is this very seminary training. It belongs to the 17th century. It is useless for the 20th. Let me quote from a recent number of the *Giornale d'Italia* some words of a distinguished French Catholic theologian which exactly express what is needed. " The priest who lives in a democratic society in which everything is questioned, who wishes to reconquer to the faith a nation which has lost it as it were out of its inner system, must acquire other qualities than the priest who lived in a monarchy and peacefully administered a wealthy parish of the faithful." And *àpropos* of this very matter, he adds, in words which no outsider would have the right of himself to use :—" The Church must be satisfied with a little band of apostles rather than seek a multitude of bureaucrats and hirelings."

The future is not perhaps bright. But at any rate it is the same future which the Church has to face everywhere. The inner conditions of character and outlook with which she must everywhere set herself to the accomplishment of her new mission are the same. And the outer conditions under which she will be called upon to undertake it will, sooner or later, be also the same. They are conditions classically defined in the words with which the dying Cavour turned in farewell to the friar who had just administered to him the last Sacraments, words which resumed the hopes and efforts of his own life :— " *Frate, libera Chiesa in libero Stato.*"

CHAPTER VIII

THE CHURCH OF ENGLAND AND THE CHURCH
OF FRANCE

May,
1907 IT is not so many years ago that any assimilation of the
problems to be faced by the Church in France and in
England would have seemed in the last degree far-fetched,
and even absurd. In those days, to begin with, we
knew little of each other. M. Thureau Dangin and
M. Bremond had not as yet made the Catholic witness
and aspiration of Anglicanism familiar to the cultivated
French public. Even M. Portal and Lord Halifax had
hardly begun to shape their generous project of an
ecclesiastical Channel tunnel which, like its political
counterpart, was so soon to learn from the peremptory
voice of authority how premature it was. And if France
knew little of ecclesiastical England, we knew just as
little of ecclesiastical France. I well remember how,
some fifteen years ago, the mild apologetic of Mgr.
Bougaud and of the Abbé de Broglie seemed to me
instances of an unhoped-for open-mindedness in the
writings of Catholic theologians. I little knew that the
Catholic Institute of Paris was already big with the
promise of a new and vigorous Catholic enlightenment.
But the past twelve years, and especially the last five,
have wrought a conspicuous change. Theological scholarship has become internationalised in an increasing degree

and at something like a popular level of intelligence. The cordial understandings so successful and so full of happy augury in the political sphere have found their parallels in the sphere of religion. Men so eminent and so influential in our own Church life as the Dean of Westminster and the Bishop of Birmingham have become the centres of a lively and very healthy interest in the fortunes of the Church of France and in those who are making its fortunes. Those " Merchants of light " whom Bacon desired to see trafficking overseas in the interests of science, now cross and recross the Channel continually in the interests of religion. It is a revolution which is being wrought, one of those silent revolutions which accomplish their work before its scope has been measured or its meaning grasped.

And perhaps the most unexpected result of this change is a very simple one. It is the discovery that the problems which religion has to solve at the moment, at least throughout Christendom, are everywhere the same. Those problems may present themselves with much local variety of detail, but their essential features recur with an almost monotonous persistence. The religious situation in France, for instance, is with but slight modifications, modifications much slighter and less important than we think, the religious situation in England, America, and Germany as well. It is well, therefore, that when that situation becomes anywhere acutely relieved on a background of menacing circumstance, we should examine it closely. For it is to some extent our own, even though in our case the menace of circumstance be less fearful or less imminent. If the fire has broken out on our neighbour's premises, let us take thought for our own.

Jam proximus ardet

Ucalegon.

It is, it must be admitted, pardonable if we have not realized this similarity of conditions in the religious sphere before. For it is only in quite recent times that it has begun to obtain. So long as the great masses of the population in every Christian land were submissive to the teaching and discipline of the Church, the problems which occupied the attention of the various religious societies were either problems peculiar to their own local circumstances or problems arising out of their theological differences with one another. They were problems which either left the Churches enclosed within their own separate paddocks or insisted that if they were to meet it must be on the battlefield. But new conditions have raised new problems. And as the new conditions are the same for all, so the new problems are the same for all. It is these new conditions which we are just beginning to scrutinize. We find that we are no longer able, any of us, to count on the submissiveness to ecclesiastical teaching and discipline of the great masses of nominally, even perhaps really, Christian people. In France, as in England, the vast majority of the people stand aloof from the Church as from an institution which is foreign to their interests and their way of regarding life. No more there than here are they hostile to religion as such. But organized religion seems to them, there as here, something unfamiliar and vaguely hostile. There as here they resort to the Church for the consecration of the great moments of the individual life—baptism, first Communion, marriage, death. But outside these occasions the Church means nothing to them. They do not seem to be even uncomfortably conscious of its presence in their midst. Its protest has no power to disturb them. And yet, as I have said, they are not actively irreligious. The number of convinced atheists is small. There is everywhere a very general belief in God as a universal Providence and as an eternal Judge. Their religion is the practical religion of simple people. It has no interest in the metaphysical subtleties of dogma, and none in the curious refinements of devotion. It was so even while attendance at Mass was a fairly universal religious custom. It is so now that that has in many places almost entirely ceased to be a custom. So far the change in real religious feeling is by no means considerable. But most of us, I think, will feel that even this simple religious belief cannot long survive the habitual divorce of Church and people.

And here is to be noted one of those local differences between the religious condition of France and England which have a real importance. In England religious feeling has been so trained in the habit of independence that, when it finds itself out of sympathy with the Church, it finds or makes for itself a new home. The theology of dissent, even in its most angular forms, is the theology of the popular intelligence. And if the religion of dissent is gradually becoming less theological and more distinctly practical, it is only reflecting the changing attitude of the people. And when no existing form of dissent is able to satisfy certain sections of our people, they do not cease to be religious nor are they willing to forego the benefits which association offers to the religious life. On the contrary they forthwith form Labour Churches, or league themselves together in some such loose religious brotherhood. But in France there is no such outlet for the dissatisfaction of the religiously inclined with the traditional Christian society. As a great French Archbishop is reported to have said recently in reply to the question whether the Separation Law was likely to lead to a schism : "There is not religion enough in France to make a schism." Under the keen French irony of the answer there lurks a great truth. The religious training of the Frenchman has made it next to impossible for him to entertain the idea of independent religious organization. Perhaps after all it is the grace of Catholicism, its special virtue, that still works in him there. Something of the old feeling for the ideal of religious unity clings about him still. But if this grace of the Church has thus robbed him of the power of independent action in matters of religion, it is the more incumbent upon her to see that he never needs to become independent of her. It is the more necessary for her to understand the signs of the times so that there may be no occasion for men of the times to abandon her unity for the outer void. If she has trained her children to believe in unity as the first of religious necessities, then she ought to be equal to the continuous development of a unity which will be adequate to the needs of religious mankind.

And here, indeed, lies the actual weakness of the Church. Like all established forces, she has come to forget that she was made for men, and to believe that men were made for her. She has rooted herself in an inflexible opposition to the two great forces of the modern world, democracy and science. Even where, as here in England, her opposition to these forces has been hesitant and wavering, it has still left the impression of hostility and fear. And nothing can be more disastrous than timid opposition ending in half-hearted concession. What was necessary in order that the Church might be true to her mission was a courageous and sympathetic attempt to understand the active and living forces of the time. Even before she could measure the scope of their action or estimate the exact character of their influence, her faith ought to have taught her that the very fact that they were living forces commended them to her sympathy and intelligence. The word of God, which the Church has been specially set to learn in order that she may teach it again, is given in living experience and in all the movements and hopes to which that experience instinctively points. It is hers, in virtue of that directive spirit which is her eternal dower, to probe these workings of a Divine instinct in the general life of man, and to extract from them their essential and permanent lessons. For those lessons are the growing revelation of God which only she can unfold, which at the very least she has been appointed by God to unfold.

Now the special interest of the crisis through which the French Church is passing is that it brings into a clear light the dangers to which the Church is everywhere exposed, and the measure and character of the Church's failure which has exposed her to those dangers. The French habit of mind is logical. It tends to carry to a

definite conclusion the tendencies which are at work in
it. Indeed, the same may be said of all the Latin races,
and it is the fact that the Roman Church represents in
the main the religion of the Latin races that has made it
the victim of a false logic—I mean of the logic of a false
position. And here let me say that when the Roman
Church turns to meet sympathetically the living forces
of to-day, as already many of her noblest and greatest
sons are doing for themselves and trying to teach her to
do, she will in virtue of that logic inherent in the races
she spiritually controls move much faster and farther in
the direction of the new truth which is opening before
the whole religious world than any other part of that
world. But meanwhile her logic has made her present
official attitude the most hopeless and reactionary in
Christendom, and the French Church has suffered from
thoughtlessly committing herself to that attitude in a
country which has done more than any other to give
consistency and force to the modern spirit. Let us take
the two forms in which this spirit has expressed itself,
and consider the attitude of the Church with regard
to them. The first is the principle of democracy,
democracy in its widest sense, the government of the
people—to use once more the hackneyed definition—by
the people, for the people. That principle was banned
and anathematised by the Syllabus of 1864. It is the
outstanding accomplishment of the pontificate of Pius IX.
To the spirit of that document the French Church has
been fatally faithful. Ever since 1870, her one effort
has been to overthrow the Republic or to undermine it
by a sinister and intriguing policy. ʃShe has allowed

herself to become the ally of a desperate and discredited political party. She resisted a democratic measure for the establishment of a national system of education in France with vehement denunciation, and filled the European press with her outcries against an atheist government. I remember how I thought in the early Eighties that France was a country of atheists, and that M. Ferry, whom the Catholic press now occasionally claims as a Liberal statesman, was the head and front of a great conspiracy to banish the name of God from the minds of Frenchmen. And all the time she was covering the face of France with the houses of religious orders which the laws passed by the Catholic monarchy had refused to authorize, and establishing, with the easy-going tolerance of a Republican Government, a vast and powerful religious militia pledged to wreck the Republic itself by all the crooked and underhand intrigues which are possible only to a spiritual power. And when this same spiritual power,* existing on extra-legal sufferance, had worked its crowning infamy and disgraced the fair name of France before the whole civilized world, the Church raised more vehemently than ever the cry of persecution because France, having come to herself, was minded to eliminate the poison from her system. That is the political record of the Church in France during the last thirty odd years. It is that record, and that record alone, that has put an end to her semi-political existence.

Is it necessary for me to point out the danger to which the Church in England exposes herself by even appearing

---

* It is, of course, the Religious Orders that are referred to.

to be the subservient ally of one political party or political order ? When the House of Lords and the Tory Party can always count on the blind support of the Church for their measures and their policy, or even when the country thinks that that is the state of things, is it well with us ? Of course I know how different are the degrees of backsliding in the two countries. It is impossible that the measure of criminal stupidity should be so great with us for two reasons: first, because any possible political alliance in this country must be with one of the recognized political parties which work our constitutional machine, and not with a party whose sole object is to subvert the existing constitution; and secondly, because the Church here has no one centre of authority, and no centre of authority at all outside the limits of the national will. Here we may have bishops like Dr. Perceval and Dr. Gore, who are often to be found on the side of popular right, and whose individual authority in that matter may be claimed as the voice of the Church with as much justice as the individual authority of other bishops. Yet we reckon authority in this country in the last resort by count of heads, and it is a standing weakness for the Church that its authority so measured is consistently pledged to one political party. The inevitable result of this attitude is disestablishment, and it is an extraordinary witness to the political patience of Englishmen that disestablishment has not come long since. Of course you will understand that I do not think of disestablishment, either for the Church of England or for the Church of France, as a curse, but as a blessing. But in both countries the Church has acted so as to draw down its imagined curse upon its own head. In France it has descended. In England it will sooner or later descend.

And would that all the consequences of reaction were as little harmful as this. But that, alas! is far from being the case. What is really dangerous in such policy is not the mere blind alliance of the Church with the fortunes of a political party, even a reactionary one. It is the transparency of the motive which has produced that alliance. The Church is afraid of the new life which is surging up among all Western peoples, and she is afraid of it not for cowardly reasons, not through fears for her temporal fortunes. It is to her credit that never in her history was she less swayed by concern for temporal goods. But that, alas! is not counted to her for righteousness with the multitude. For instinctively the multitude feels that she is afraid of life itself, that she shrinks from trusting it as the medium of a revelation of things that are true and things that are honourable. And there the multitude is right. She has lost faith in the revelation of God through history. She wants to hold the present and the future in the leading-strings of the past. She has become for the multitude a spiritual mother or grandmother, whom it venerates still, but to whose apron-strings it will not be tied. The democracies, thrilled with the vigorous lust of life, need more than ever the guide which could help them to sift the inspiration of the new forces and ideas, to prove the untried spirits whose possession intoxicates them. And the old guide has failed them. She distrusts all the spirits because they are new, because they do not yield to the traditional tests which she has been accustomed to apply. She preaches her doctrine of renunciation and submission as if it could serve an age which is stung by a kind of Dionysiac rage of life. And, finding that her preaching of such doctrines is vain, she entrenches herself more firmly than ever in a mood of defiant authority.

Here, again, of course, it is quite true that the Church of England has not offended so deeply as the Church of Rome. Indeed, it would be more true to say that English, or rather Teutonic religion, whether Roman, Anglican, or Protestant, has not offended so deeply in this regard as Latin religion. It is a matter of national temperament rather than of the idiosyncrasies of different religious societies. The Teutonic races have always cultivated the active virtues more efficiently than the passive, and therefore in an age which demands action and faith in action, their religion is less endangered. But even with us there is a certain suspicion of independent thought and action, a certain exaltation of the virtues of submission and obedience which is of doubtful efficacy in our present conditions. The note of undiscriminating authority is too often sounded by the official voice of the Church. At any rate the honest lay thinker has come to feel that he cannot look to the Church for any sympathy with or intelligence of his labour. He never thinks of submitting his treasures to the Church for her judgment upon them. When his enquiries land him in difficulties which rend the heart or cloud the spirit, he takes it for granted that the Church will pass him by on the other side. They are not the kind of difficulties, he thinks, to which she will have any answer.

But I am already encroaching upon the second expression of the modern spirit to which the Church has proved herself unsympathetic. Once the Church was the focus of the scientific movement among men, the leader and guide of man's attempt to know. She must again become such. St. Thomas was the greatest of Christian teachers because he was the supreme master of all the science of the Middle Age. The Church will not be herself again till she has produced a new St. Thomas, another master of both the analytic and the synthetic method as great as he was. But meanwhile the only analysis which finds any favour among orthodox theologians is a purely dialectical analysis, the analysis of the mathematician, the logical exposition of the contents of a given thesis. And of synthesis the ordinary theologian does not even admit the need. For him the final religious synthesis was reached long ago. Truth is a sealed book, or at least a book the last page of which has been written. And this in an age when the human mind is feverishly engaged in forming provisional syntheses of the most various and contradictory character! The Church ought to be in the thick of the fray, disengaging whatever of new and vital truth there may be in all this fever of speculation through the power of that spirit of life and truth which possesses her. But instead she is laying the dead hand of authority on all speculation and rebuking it with her " *non possumus.*" And for this supreme folly, and indeed supreme dereliction of one of her essential duties, the Church of France has conspicuously suffered. It was inevitable that it should be so. There is no country in the world where intellectual activity is more general, or, I may add, more thorough and sincere. In such a country to disregard the problems of thought is to be condemned beforehand to futility and powerlessness. And the Church has not merely disregarded them, but brushed them impatiently aside as unworthy of her attention, and condemned their provisional solutions as soul-destroying heresies. Meanwhile she has buttressed herself on her self-chosen ground of devotion, with the result that she has shut out from her pale all but the unintelligently devout and a few of those steadfast and loyal souls who will not be repulsed by her coldness or her suspicion of their independent mental attitude. For the little coterie of the devout she invents new marvels of devotion every day, divorcing herself and the cause of religion which she has in charge with increasing certainty from the intelligence of the time. This routine of a devotion which becomes more and more superstitious is growing to be the sole word of religion which the Church has to utter to a spiritually distracted age. The devout secure all her favours ; they practically direct, or rather dictate, her policy. They run her newspapers and speak her mind to a world which can afford to smile at the fatuous stupidity of it all. And when the intelligent clergy protest at such a prostitution of the function of the greatest of all human teachers, they are met with the thunders of the *Osservatore Romano* and official denunciation of their unorthodoxy or disloyalty.

I think we can recognize some of these dangers, again I hope in a lesser degree, among ourselves. The narrowing of the Church to a little circle of what I may call experts

in devotion ; the practical excommunication of the
common people who would hear the word gladly if it
were expressed in symbols which they could understand,
but who know nothing of and care nothing for outlandish
types of devotion ; the dreary fuss of the clergy over
minute points of ritual and adornment which minister
only to religious priggishness in youths and maidens at
an age when priggishness is a danger and religious priggishness a special danger ; the religious dictatorship of a
little knot of ecclesiastical laymen ; that arrogant and
omniscient tone which is too often adopted by our
clerical press—these are some of the ways in which we
have all unconsciously reproduced that situation in
France, against which all the noblest spirits of the
French clergy are strenuously fighting.

And think of why all this has come about. It has
come about through a false exaltation of the Church
which has belittled the Church, as all self-assertion and
self-importance always does. She is here, beyond our
praise or our blame, independently of our exaltation or
our neglect. She is here, with the Divine Spirit eternally
in her heart ; here, accredited with that divinest of
missions—to serve humanity ; here, set to listen for the
word of truth and capture its harmony as it breaks in
rude discords through the agelong experience of humanity;
here, to be present to every sincere endeavour after truth
and right, recognizing it for her own and consecrating it
for the life of the future with her sanctions ; here, just
as she has come to us, her face marred and bruised more
than any man's, out of the long warfare against evil
which she has fought without flinching ; here, in the

variety of her human experience and the manifold wisdom of her human methods; here, in the seamless robe of her Divine purpose; here, One, Holy, Catholic, Apostolic, in her spirit. And we have found nothing better to do than to sterilise her will and her redemptive effort by forcing her for a generation to demonstrate about herself and to flaunt all her credentials—and those not always even genuine ones—in the face of a scoffing world. This is what the best sons of France have been proclaiming for a decade to be the recusancy of the Church of to-day, and the cause of her present bankruptcy. I fear that some part of the indictment applies to ourselves.

CHAPTER IX

THE SYLLABUS OF THEOLOGICAL ERRORS

THE Decree, *Lamentabili Sane,* of the Holy Roman and *September, 1907* Universal Inquisition, to which an apt historical reminiscence has already, whether legitimately or not, given the popular title, " The Syllabus of Pius X," is a document whose immediate and obvious interest is naturally for members of the Roman Communion only. But from many points of view it is inevitable that the attention of the whole Christian world should be held by the judgments of so imposing a tribunal. The curiosity which provokes to interest in our neighbour's affairs is not always idle or malign. It may sometimes be the honest and humble recognition of the risks of a common adventure.

And assuredly in the present crisis of theological speculation throughout Christendom such risks are both numerous and formidable. The Christian theologian of to-day is a seeker in a new intellectual region. Vast unfamiliar spaces surround him. The pioneers of science and history are daily bringing in their reports of the new lands which he must subdue to the familiar uses of human habitation. The climate tries him by its strangeness, and even more by its savage and unhumanised rawness. The rank natural growths which surround him are charged with a deadly poison to which he must find an immediate antidote, with an unconscious malice which

247

his skill must speedily exorcize. He must fell, clear, subdue, transform. It is his to humanise a new world, to make a new spiritual home for men in the midst of strange conditions. He has the old faith to work with, the faith that in himself and his fellow-men is revealed, both as need and power, and to some degree as knowledge proceeding from that need and power, the essential character of the ideal spiritual city. That faith he brings with him as a living tradition from the old home he has had to abandon, from the old familiar world which he will never forget, but in which he will never live again. He must fit it somehow to this new world into which he has come. He must subdue all these new natural forces into its service. He has no least shadow of doubt that these forces exist only to be subdued by him to this end. He knows the risks and dangers of such an enterprise, but he knows also that those risks must be faced, those dangers met. He knows that there is only one course which is absolutely fatal—to pretend that there are no risks, that this new uncouth world needs no subdual, to insist and to hypnotise himself by his insistence into believing that he is in his old world still, and that all will be well if only everyone else will believe as he does.

The Christian theologian, then, who has realized the new situation is under no illusion. He knows that his mission is a dangerous one, but he knows too that the danger of declining it, or of pretending that no exceptional mission is necessary, is infinitely greater. And in facing these new problems, in undertaking this unfamiliar mission, he has made a discovery which alleviates his sense of danger, which at least heartens him to meet all possible perils of the enterprise.   It is that in this new land of the spirit his ancient theological enemies are pledged of necessity to the same adventure with himself. They are both moving forward in faith to the conquest and ordering of the unknown.   A sense of comradeship, distant as yet and formally unrecognized, but nevertheless strong in the growing consciousness of the common task, is gaining hold upon the ancient foes.   Each of the pioneering bands watches with interest the dispositions of the other, and with something that is near to sympathy its measure of success.

It is on this account that those who are not of the Roman Communion are interested in this new Syllabus of theological errors.   We have for years followed with increasing sympathy the efforts of the Roman pioneers to clear a passable track for the spirit through the tangled undergrowth of that new intellectual world in which we have all suddenly found ourselves.   Our sympathy has been the greater in that we recognized the more arduous nature of the conditions under which they laboured.   Attached to an army in which the necessary discipline of the camp had hardened through ages into the formal and hampering punctilio of the court, they yet strove with a quiet dignity and a tenacious courage to persuade etiquette out of its formal scruples and into a realization of the nature and magnitude of the task in hand.   And now we understand that this Syllabus is the deliberate and long-pondered judgment of Roman authority upon their efforts.   The day of the mere pioneer is past.   His work, which is always necessary, has been accomplished.   His report has been received at headquarters and solemnly considered. We are now to hear the general order founded upon that report, in obedience to which the whole army will move.

For many who have not closely followed the Liberal movement in the Roman Church, the first interest of the Syllabus will be its authoritative revelation of the actual positions held by the present-day theological pioneers of that Church. They have heard, perhaps, vaguely of certain alleged audacities of theological renewal on the part of a few Roman writers. The names of Tyrrell and of Loisy may have filtered through the distorting medium of newspaper clamour, and have thus come to symbolize some fantastic mood of revolt or reform in Rome, they know not which, and they care perhaps as little to know. If they are intelligent and educated laymen, they have long since lost all interest in that weaving of ropes out of sand which they have found modern theology to be. And they are mildly amused at the assumption which all this fuss about Roman Liberalism implies, that one more desperate attempt at flogging the dead horse of theology into a painful semblance of life can possibly interest them. No doubt, they think, it is nothing more than a new sleight-of-hand trick which some of these amazingly clever Roman jugglers have invented to revive the jaded attention of a sceptical public. Well, if that is their thought, let them buy a copy of the *Tablet* of July 27th, and see what the Roman Congregation of the Inquisition accuses these men of actually teaching. They will find there sixty-five propositions, precise and categorical in their form, representing, according to this authoritative guardian of Christian truth, "errors which are being daily spread among the faithful." And though those who know most about the movement of which I am speaking may fail to recognize some of these "errors" as the actual teaching of its leaders, yet, lest there should be any doubt, the Roman correspondent of the *Tablet* tells us in the same number that he "has been asked to emphasize the fact that the errors condemned in the Syllabus are precisely those that are being taught and spread, and that the propositions containing them are contained actually and not merely constructively or deductively in the writings from which they have been taken." Now there is no indication, either in the Syllabus itself or in any of the more or less official comments upon it which I have read (and I have read many, both in Italian, in French, and in English), that any of the condemned propositions have been taken from non-Roman writers. The Syllabus has therefore, through the medium of the highest official authority, summarised for us the actual theological speculation of modern Liberal Roman writers. It is no small service for a busy public whose interest in these matters needs the stimulus of vivid simplification, even if that simplification happens to be unfair, or in some instances (see Propositions 19 and 65) grotesque. The outstanding and, we may hope, fruitful result of this resounding condemnation of the Roman Inquisition is that the whole world may now know that the problems which face Christian faith everywhere are being felt with the same force in the Roman Communion as they are felt outside it, and have provoked attempts at solution as fearless and far-reaching as any which have been ventured by the boldest free lances of the most unfettered of Christian Communions.

We are thus enabled, on the authority of the Roman Church itself, to test the value of its boasted doctrine of Infallibility. Here are men whose devotion to the Roman Church cannot be questioned, who have suffered much through their devotion to it, and have yet, we fear, to suffer much more, and yet whose attempt to think out what the Christian faith means has forced them at the very least to recognize that the problems which Christian faith has now to solve are exactly such as the ordinary Christian without any infallible guidance finds them to be, has forced them further to solutions which do not seem appreciably to differ from those reached by fallible private judgment. Never surely had a Church, whose infallibility has been for nearly forty years an article of faith, such an opportunity of justifying her crowning act of belief in her Divine guidance as has been accorded to Rome during that period of intellectual revolution which has been almost exactly coeval with her own declared power to meet it. Yet the total result is that those of her sons who have been most intellectually alive, and who have devoted their intellect to the resolution of difficulties which none can escape, are in no better plight than the unprotected victims of private judgment, and have received at the end for all their pains the *coup de bâton* of official authority.

Again Rome has spoken. And what has she said? Not one word of enlightenment upon a situation the most intricate and perilous. She has simply condemned sixty-five propositions, " characterized " (as the *Tablet* tells us) " by that precision of expression in which Rome excels, which the Latin language is so well adapted to convey." And yet even of this merit of precise expression, save in so far as it is exhibited in translation into the Latin language, the Roman correspondent of the same journal cruelly robs her, since he " has been asked to emphasize the fact " that the condemned propositions are " contained actually in the writings from which they have been taken." All these sixty-five propositions have grown out of a sincere attempt to deal with difficulties which no thinking mind in our time can escape. Yet they are condemned, and there is an end. We are left where we were. No sign reaches us of sympathy with or understanding of the new situation which has arisen. Do the Roman authorities think that we are living still in pre-Copernican, pre-Darwinian, pre-Niebuhrian days ? Or do they know perfectly well that we are not, and yet refuse to do anything to acclimatize the eternal Christian faith in the changed world in which, by grace or evil craft of the masters of modern astronomy, of modern science, of the modern historical method, we are privileged or compelled to live ? Apparently it is not the part of an infallible authority to teach its children, who have begun to feel that they have legs and that there is a real solid earth beneath them upon which perhaps those legs were meant to find the delight of their own power, how to walk safely and warily. At any rate it confines itself to a futile scolding of the adventurous children who are clumsily trying to use their legs as best they can, and to a coaxing recommendation to the others to remain for ever in their comfortable cradle. Or, to use the words of the author of a recent Open Letter to the Pope,* "Authority, incapable of entering into the spirit and understanding the writings of its faithful and deserving servants, does not confute, does not discuss, but condemns, and condemns because it does not understand."

But this Syllabus is not merely a condemnation. It is a travesty, and by reason of that very "precision of expression which the Latin language is so well adapted to convey." The *Tablet* is evidently delighted with these "short paragraphs in the Latin text of the Decree" which have sublimated the poison so discreetly diffused in "lengthy passages of flowing Italian, or brilliant French, or refined yet strangely puzzling English." Now poison is not poison until it is concentrated. It exists, I believe, as a natural and healthy constituent in most of the substances we usually eat and cannot well refrain from eating unless we are to perish. It is only when it is concentrated that it becomes dangerous, that it is what we call poison at all. And these sixty-five propositions constitute a travesty of Liberal Roman speculation, just because the "short Latin paragraphs" in which they are set forth are such a concentration. I say this, remembering well that they are alleged to be "contained actually in the writings from which they have been taken." That may be perfectly true, though my knowledge of the writings from which presumably the condemned propositions have been drawn, and it is a fairly wide one, does not

* "What we Want. An Open Letter to Pius X." John Murray. 1907.

always enable me to find these propositions "actually contained" in them. But apart from this altogether, the Syllabus is a travesty of the teaching of Roman Liberals. I can imagine a Roman Liberal signing wholeheartedly, if not all, yet many of these condemnations. For what has been done? From apologetic writings whose very essence is the accommodation of the Christian faith to altogether novel conditions of thought and knowledge, whose force lies in a careful attempt at discrimination of elements which were formerly held to be indissolubly fused together, whose validity depends upon the qualifications and reserves which a complex subject-matter demanded and which these writings actually contained, certain crude and unrelieved propositions have been excerpted and submitted for condemnation in short paragraphs of that Latin language which is so remarkable for its capacity of precise expression. Is it possible to conceive of any means less likely to secure the truth or to condemn error? After such a process, we are as much in the dark as ever as to where truth may lie or even as to where exactly error lurks. The error which is condemned is a pure abstraction, far indeed from that concrete error which may still linger undetected and unreproved in the minds and writings of these victims of infallible incapacity. That word returns to us: "Authority condemns because it does not understand."

And its want of understanding is the real danger which still has to be faced. This Syllabus confuses, or refuses to recognize, the real issue. It still dumps down, without a word of explanation, without a hint that it realizes any need of explanation, the faith-cum-science construction of an entirely past habit of mind. But there is a new science, a new history, a new psychology. The universe, human development, the individual soul, have been revealed to us under new forms. We understand them all, or try to understand them, under new categories. There must be a new fusion of the ancient faith with this new science. And that fusion will take place of itself when, and it cannot take place until, one piece of honest work has been done. It waits until the analysis of the old faith-cum-science construction has been completed. And it is the honest acceptance of the results, even if provisional, of the new science (the results of any real science are always provisional), and above all the profound penetration of the contemporary mind by its presuppositions and methods, that can alone bring about the completion of that analysis. Meanwhile its progress is sufficiently advanced to enable at least some of us to surmise the forms which faith in God and in Christ must inevitably take in some not distant future. Those forms will be determined, as they always have been determined in every living epoch of Christian thought, by what men actually know of themselves and of the world, not by some abstract metaphysic crowned with whatever halo of traditional glory. The sixty-five condemned propositions of the new Syllabus, travesty as they may be and most certainly, in their detached crudity, are of the teaching of Liberal Roman theologians, are after all valuable in that they reveal through all their crudity how far the freshest and most vigorous minds of the Church of Rome have gone towards recognizing the necessity, and even suggesting the actual outlines of these forms. No other value can well be accorded this document, except perhaps this—that it is one more demonstration of the practical futility and the theoretical absurdity of what orthodox Roman theologians call Infallibility. They are careful indeed to tell us beforehand that this document is not infallible, but they insist that it is nevertheless " binding upon Catholics in the sense that they must acquiesce in the teaching therein contained with an assent at once full, perfect, and absolute." A new device, I suppose, for claiming all the advantages, without incurring any of the risks, of œcumenical decisions ! But the plain outsider expects Infallibility to be really infallible by clearly proclaiming the truth when the dangers of error are so great and unavoidable. He is, as usual, disappointed, and the Syllabus of Pius X goes the way of that of Pius IX—to the limbo of things forgotten and contemned.

CHAPTER X

THE ENCYCLICAL "PASCENDI"

December,
1907 IT is the same freakish accident of first words that gave to the world the recent decree of the Inquisition under the amusingly apt and descriptive title *Lamentabili*, and has again so ironically named the latest Papal Encyclical *Pascendi*. It is, indeed, difficult to see how Pius X can persuade himself that he has here discharged that duty of feeding the Lord's flock which has been "divinely entrusted to him." What he has done is to condemn, with every added instance of contempt and reproach, those who were attempting to lead the flock into the fresh fields and pastures new which the Lord of life had prepared for it. For himself, he has once more forbidden the flock to wander beyond the narrow pen of scholasticism where every scanty blade has long since been nibbled to its hard and sapless roots. A part of the Lord's flock is to be harried in order that the rest may be starved, or rather made content with its now habitual starvation.

It is not assuredly the condemnation of what this Encyclical presents to us, under the name of Modernism, as a closely-knit and wholly consistent intellectual scheme for the deformation of Christianity that is the most serious feature of the fatal situation it has created. Indeed this supposed Modernist *system* is but a perverse figment of the imagination of the clever and inveterately

258

scholastic theologian to whom Pius X entrusted the drafting of the Encyclical—report says of M. Billot of the Roman College of the Jesuits. No one who knows anything of the various movements co-ordinated by this writer, whoever he may have been, under the name of Modernism, can fail to detect the unfairness or wilful blindness of that lust of system-mongering which has impelled him to his task. Practical Church reformers, for instance, like Don Romolo Murri, or philosophic apologists like M. Fonsegrive, are among those whose aims and achievements the Encyclical would expressly condemn. Yet they are both of them neo-scholastics, obedient to the impulse given by the Encyclical *Æterni Patris* of Leo XIII. Again, a certain simile is quoted with impatient contempt as " that of one of the leaders of Modernism." Yet it is a simile which has been used by a distinguished English Catholic writer who has often most loyally, if somewhat subtly, defended the most disastrous excesses of Roman authority. The truth is that there is no necessary intellectual cohesion, and often none in fact, between the various movements which the Encyclical masses under a common title and a common condemnation. They have indeed a connection, but that connection is not logical, but vital. They all spring out of a common impulse of life. And that is just the reason that they are all alike condemned. Life has its risks, or rather becomes life only through incurring risks ; and Roman authority does not will that there should be any risks in religion. It wants a religion which on the side of intellectual expression will be absolutely safe ; and that, by reason of the nature of truth, means a religion that is intellectually dead. It is not an unusual, and perhaps not an unnatural, desire on the part of religious authority. Yet it is just an ancient and venerable religious authority that might have been expected, in virtue of its long experience, to free itself from the illusion of such a de. ire. God reveals His truth and His goodness through tl e activity of the human mind and will, through the quest of truth and goodness by actual living souls. So at least we thought we had learned, but His Vicegerent seems to think the notion so absurd that it is only necessary to state it to expose its absurdity.

It is not then a particular self-consistent philosophico-religious theory which is condemned by this Encyclical, but religion itself trying to express itself in its living reality along the various lines of activity which the Encyclical has chosen to group together as Modernism. For some years an immense religious revival has been seething in the bosom of the Roman Church as elsewhere ; there, indeed, perhaps more conspicuously than elsewhere. This revival has taken the general form which every far-reaching religious revival must in time assume, of seeking the Divine will and way in the most generous movements of contemporary life, or at least of seeking there their illustration and interpretation. The Christian thinker has sought for a revelation, or rather for a satisfying form of revelation, in contemporary thought. The Christian scholar has lost his fear of that revision of historical fact which unprejudiced critical enquiry seems to impose. The practical Christian has found in the active forces of contemporary life a fresh inspiration and direction of his religious hopes and aims. He would revive and fortify the spirit of the Church by modifying its antiquated and hampering forms. Above all he would remind authority of its duty of fostering and guiding life, and not allow it to content itself with merely distrusting and rebuking life. And through all this various expression of tendencies and endeavours it is a vital religious spirit that has been working. The resistless breath of life has passed upon the dry bones of use and custom, and, clad in joyous flesh and blood, they are marching to the possession of a living earth. It is just at such a moment that authority ought to find its opportunity. If it is to prove itself worthy of its rôle, it ought to place itself with confidence at the head of the living host, to welcome its ardours, to knit together its energies, to chasten if need be its headlong impulsiveness. The particular expressions of the reforming impulse are accidental, and may need correction. But at least some expression is necessary, just because life is there. And it is surely the function of any authority which can be accepted as worthy, to rescue life from the excesses of its recovered liberty, and not merely to immure it once more in the prison from which it had escaped.

Yet that seems to be in effect the response of Roman authority to this courageous attempt to renew the religious life of the Roman Church. There is not in this pronouncement of an infallible authority the slightest sign of recognition that religious faith is beset by any difficulties whatever, except indeed those which spring from the spiritual pride or the intellectual presumption of vainglorious and ignorant men. The very difficulties which they feign, they have themselves created through these moral defects. The whole sum of philosophical speculation since the days of St. Thomas is scornfully dismissed as the " ravings of philosophers." Abundant ridicule is heaped upon that conception of an inner sense of God native to the human soul by which the mystics who have adorned Rome above all other Communions habitually lived and realized their spiritual life. A crude psychology is as confidently appealed to as if no other were possible which would make a kind of absolute distinction, a distinction inherent in the nature of things, and not merely in our various manipulation of our interpenetrating faculties, between sentiment and reason. Nay, this psychology would actually antagonize the two, and regard sentiment as a kind of natural and diabolical enemy which reason has always to subjugate and control. The conception of sentiment as already charged with an inherent reason which needs to be evoked and defined, is not so much scouted as not even entertained as tenable by reasonable beings. Knowledge is not so much affirmed as confidently implied, without any need of affirmation, to be the result of the operation of reason as a separate faculty upon the data of a mechanically acting sense-perception. A deductive philosophy which, if it could be rigorously enforced, would annul every gain of science during the last three centuries by a simple demonstration of the false method which inductive science has employed, is once more enthroned on the seat of knowledge by this intellectual ukase. Religion is chained to the mummified corpse of Scholasticism preserved with considerable pomp in Roman schools for the reverent inspection of those who frequent those museums of the intellect. It is absolutely forbidden, upon pain of immediate dissolution into atheism, to have any truck with the ravings of living philosophers. This is the guidance of authority in the midst of a great religious crisis.

But this is not all, nor is it indeed the most alarming, if it is the least excusable, aspect of this intervention of authority. What is worse is that the Encyclical revives in its most arrogant and relentless form the conception of religion as mere submission—voluntary, or if need be enforced—to a closed and rigid system. It is unfortunately a conception which fits in too easily with the habits and traditions of the Latin races. It is almost impossible for the Anglo-Saxon or the Teuton, whether he be Roman, Anglican, or Protestant, to conceive how entirely religion is identified with government and order in the Latin, and especially in the Roman mind. The old imperial principle and imperial idea still dominate the life and especially the religion of these races after fifteen centuries. For them religion has always been, and still is, mainly a consecration of the social order. Attendance at Mass is still a customary social duty punctiliously observed by great masses of people who never think of " practising " their religion where it claims them as individuals. And it is just these masses who had never heard of Modernism until this Encyclical was issued, and who, having now heard of it, will immediately dismiss it from their minds with the careless reflection that " Rome has spoken," and that there is an end of some new and uncomfortable religious novelty. It is this attitude of the laity which provoked that saying of a French ecclesiastic at the time of the Separation Law, " There is not religion enough in France to make a schism." This indifference to vital religion, this disposition to regard religion as merely external order and government and decent recognition of it, will be accentuated or, if that is not possible, will be authoritatively sanctioned by this decision. Meanwhile there has to be considered its effect upon the small but vastly important intellectual *élite* among the laity, the men of University training who are familiar with the mind of their generation, and who, just because of that familiarity, have been drawn to a serious interest in religion and even to a devout and earnest " practice " of it. It is they and a large section of the younger clergy in France and Northern Italy, and even in Sicily—those who ought to know are bold enough to say a majority of them—who will be straitened in mind and spirit by this action of authority. They had dreamed of a Catholicism which would be worthy of that great name, which was about to conquer and subdue its essentially schismatic mood of a moment, even if that moment had counted as four centuries. And here they find themselves flung back upon a mood wilfully uncatholic and sectarian, upon a mood which would definitely divorce their Church from the living world and enclose it for ever within fenced walls. Every device of an organized spiritual police is to be employed to procure an absolute docility and the unmurmuring silence of death within the world-defying walls of the spiritual city. *Perinde ac cadaver* is to be extended from the Society of Jesus to the whole Church as its sufficient and compelling motto. And this corpse-like submission is to be achieved by teaching the clergy to think as nobody in the evil world can any longer think ; by extending the Inquisition (which has, says a Roman Cardinal, justified itself by keeping Spain Catholic !) to every diocese ; by guarding the faithful from the injury of inoculation with the poison of Modernist literature—an injury "greater than that caused by immoral reading " ; by Episcopal policing of Catholic booksellers ; by snatching from the hands of the faithful (the *Tablet* mildly translates "put out of reach of the faithful," but the inimitable Latin language is more pregnant with its "*e manibus fidelium auferre* ")* every injurious book ; by removing Modernist professors from their chairs and setting them to menial work ; by a censorship so universal and efficient that no "bad book " (*i.e.*, Modernist writing) may henceforth succeed in getting printed ; by preventing the clergy from meeting to discuss anything that ought to interest them, especially their Bishops and the Apostolic See ; finally, by a perpetual and universal system of delation whereby everything done throughout the universal world shall be whispered in the secret chamber at Rome. The Pope has exclaimed in a lyrical outburst of horror : "*Procul, procul esto a sacro ordine novitatum amor.*" If he had only been less afraid of novelty, the telephone or even the Marconigraph might have been redeemed to high spiritual uses.

Yet it may be safely predicted that this gigantic scheme of spiritual police will fail of its object, and fail

* It ought to be stated that the Encyclical quotes this gem from Leo XIII's Apostolic Constitution *Officiorum*; but how delightedly it must have adopted it and turned it to its own account.

too of that which assuredly cannot be its object, but
would nevertheless be its inevitable effect if it succeeded,
—the annihilation of the Roman Church as an effective
spiritual force in the world.   It will not succeed because
the men against whom it is directed are inspired by an
intense religious zeal   and   sustained   by   an intense
religious faith, and because their zeal and their faith are
alike fed by their communion with the Roman See as the
centre of the living religious tradition of Christendom.
If religious tradition meant for them something intellectual, the right holding of a particular interpretation
of the faith, then that communion might not be necessary
to their spiritual life.   But the tradition which they find
most fully illustrated in Rome is the tradition of the
religious experience of innumerable saintly souls. From
that spiritual communion nothing, not even formal
excommunication at the hands of Roman authority,
can or will separate them. Father Tyrrell has just
explained their attitude and determination with his usual
clearness and strength in the pages of the *Grande Revue.**
And if, to entertain for a moment what I believe to be
the impossible, Rome should succeed in forcing them at
last out of that measure of faithfulness to her which
alone she will permit, then one of two things will happen.
Either she will continue in her obstinate blindness, and
there will be an end of her spiritual dominion, or she will
hasten once again to build the tombs of her martyred
prophets and to reform herself on the lines which their
prophecy had marked out and their martyrdom deepened.
Meanwhile, wherever the Catholic temper is alive in

* October   10,   1907.   Article   entitled, "L'Excommunication
Salutaire."

Christendom, these men will be honoured for their faithfulness to the Catholic ideal. It is only where the decaying remains of a merely sectarian Protestantism still fester as a rival and response to the unsavoury sectarianism of the present mood of Roman authority, that they are greeted with the unintelligent and unchivalrous cry, " Serve you right ; what business have you there ? " Thus it is that unbridled absolutism and unbridled individualism induce the same sectarian temper and proclaim with the same assurance the necessity on the one hand of compelling all to accept the same intellectual expression of religious experience, and on the other of dividing over every expression of it which may commend itself to the individual mind.

BIBLIOGRAPHY

(a) WORKS NOTICED IN THIS VOLUME

DENIS (l'Abbé CHARLES). *L'Église et l'État : Les Leçons de l'Heure Présente.* Paris, Roger et Chernoviz, 1902.

HOGAN, J., P.S.S. *Les Études du Clergé,* traduit de l'Anglais par l'Abbé A. Boudinhon. Paris, Lethielleux, 1901.

MIGNOT (Mgr. F. I., Archevêque d'Albi). *La Méthode de la Théologie.* Discours pour la séance de rentrée de l'Institut Catholique de Toulouse (13 Nov., 1901). Paris, Lecoffre, 1902.

—— *The Method of Theology* (English translation of above). Catholic Truth Society, 1902.

HOUTIN (l'Abbé ALBERT). *La Question Biblique chez les Catholiques de France au XIXe. Siècle.* Paris, Picard et fils, 1902.

—— *L'Américanisme.* Paris, Nourry, 1904.

LOISY (l'Abbé ALFRED). *L'Évangile et l'Église.* Paris, Picard et fils, 1902.

—— *The Gospel and the Church* (English translation of above). Pitman, 1903.

—— *Autour d'un Petit Livre.* Paris, Picard et fils, 1903.

DESJARDINS (PAUL). *Catholicisme et Critique.* Paris, Cahiers de la Quinzaine, 1905.

LABERTHONNIÈRE (le Père L., de l'Oratoire). *Essais de Philosophie Religieuse.* Paris, Lethielleux, 1903.

VON HÜGEL (Baron FRIEDRICH). *Du Christ Éternel et de nos Christologies Successives.* Extrait de *La Quinzaine,* June 1, 1904.

Lettres Romaines. Paris, Roger et Chernoviz. Extrait des *Annales de Philosophie Chrétienne,* 1904.

FOGAZZARO (ANTONIO). *Il Santo.* Milano, Baldini Castoldi e Co., 1906.

BRIGGS (Rev. CHARLES A.), and VON HÜGEL (Baron FRIEDRICH). *The Papal Commission and the Pentateuch.* London, Longmans, 1906.

LE ROY (ÉDOUARD). *Dogme et Critique.* Paris, Bloud et Cie., 1907.

269

(b) OTHER WORKS OF, OR ABOUT, LIBERAL
CATHOLIC THEOLOGY

TYRRELL (GEORGE). *Lex Orandi.* Longmans, 1903.
—— *Lex Credendi.* Longmans, 1906.
—— *Oil and Wine.* Longmans, 1906.
—— *A Much-abused Letter.* Longmans, 1906.
—— *Through Scylla and Charybdis.* Longmans, 1907.
—— Two articles in the *Times* (Sept. 30 and Oct. 1, 1907) on the
    Encyclical " Pascendi."
—— *The Prospects of Modernism.* HIBBERT JOURNAL, Jan., 1908.
TYRRELL (GEORGE) and PETRE (M.D.). *The Soul's Orbit.* Long-
    mans, 1904.
PETRE (M. D.). *Where Saints have Trod.* Catholic Truth
    Society, 1903.
—— *Catholicism and Independence.* Longmans, 1907.
WILLIAMS (W. J.). *Newman, Pascal, Loisy, and the Catholic
    Church.* FRANCIS GRIFFITHS, 1906.
PALMER (W. SCOTT). *The Church and Modern Men.* Longmans,
    1907.
HECKER (Rev. ISAAC THOMAS). *The Church and the Age.* New
    York, Catholic Book Exchange, 1896.
ELLIOTT (Rev. WALTER). *The Life of Father Hecker.* 2nd
    edition. New York, Columbus Press, 1894.
SPALDING (Mgr. J. L., Bishop of Peoria, Ill., U.S.A.). *Opportunity.*
—— *Opportunité* (traduit de l'Anglais par l'Abbé Félix Klein).
    Paris, Lethielleux, 1901.
        (This work is known to me only in the French
    translation. I have not been able to ascertain the
    name of the publisher of the American edition or the
    date of its publication, as the British Museum Library
    does not contain a copy.)
BLONDEL (MAURICE). *L'Action.* Paris, Alcan, 1893.
—— *Lettre sur les exigences de la Pensée contemporaine en matière
    d'apologétique et sur la méthode de la Philosophie dans
    l'étude du problème religieux.* (Annales de Philosophie
    Chrétienne). 1896.
MIGNOT (Mgr. E. I., Archevêque d'Albi). *Critique et Tradition,*
    extrait du *Correspondant* (10 janvier, 1904). Paris, de
    Soye et fils, 1904.
LABERTHONNIÈRE l'Abbé L.). *Le Réalisme Chrétien et l'Idéalisme
    Grec.* Paris, Lethielleux, 1904.
LABERTHONNIÈRE (l'Abbé L.)., CHEVALIER (JACQUES), et LE
    GENDRE (MAURICE). *Le Catholicisme et la Société.* Paris,
    Giard et Brière, 1907.

LE ROY (ÉDOUARD). *Comment se pose le problème de Dieu.* Extrait de la *Revue de la Métaphysique et de Morale.* Mars et juillet, 1907.
HOUTIN (l'Abbé ALBERT). *La Question Biblique au XXe Siècle.* Paris, Nourry, 1906.
—— *La Crise du Clergé.* Paris, Nourry, 1907.
SAINTYVES (P.). *La Réforme Intellectuelle du Clergé.* Paris, Nourry, 1904.
—— *Les Saints Successeurs des Dieux.* Paris, Nourry, 1907.
—— *Le Miracle et la Critique Historique.* Paris, Nourry, 1907.
—— *Le Miracle et la Critique Scientifique.* Paris, Nourry, 1907.
DIMNET (l'Abbé ERNEST). *La Pensée Catholique dans l'Angleterre Contemporaine.* Paris, Lecoffre, 1906.
DE BONNEFOY (l'Abbé JEHAN). *Les Leçons de la Défaite.* Paris, Nourry, 1907.
—— *Vers L'Unité de la Croyance.* Paris, Nourry, 1907.
—— *Le Catholicisme de Demain.* Paris, Nourry, 1908.
BREMOND (l'Abbé HENRI). *L'Inquiétude Religieuse.* Paris, Perrin, 1901.
—— *Ames Religieuses.* Paris, Perrin, 1902.
—— *Newman : Essai de Biographie Psychologique.* Paris, Bloud, 1906.
—— *The Mystery of Newman.* (English translation of above), with preface by the Rev. G. Tyrrell. Williams & Norgate, 1907.
BUREAU (PAUL). *La Crise Morale des Temps Nouveaux.* Paris, Bloud, 1907.
LE MORIN (J.). *Vérités d'Hier. La Théologie traditionnelle et les Critiques catholiques.* Paris, Nourry, 1907.
LEFRANC (E.). *Les Conflits de la Science et de la Bible.* Paris, Nourry, 1906.
MICHAUD (Dr. E.). *Les Enseignements essentiels du Christ.* Paris, Nourry, 1907.
BIROT (l'Abbé L.). *Le Mouvement Religieux.* Paris, Lecoffre, 1901.
FONSEGRIVE (GEORGE L.). *Le Catholicisme et la Vie de l'Esprit.* Paris, Lecoffre, 1899.
—— *Catholicisme et Démocratie.* Paris, Lecoffre, 1898.
—— *Lettres d'un Curé de Campagne.* Paris, Lecoffre, 1895.
—— *Lettres d'un Curé de Canton.* Paris, Lecoffre, 1895.
—— *Le Journal d'un Évêque, pendant le Concordat.* Paris, Lecoffre, 1897.
—— *Le Journal d'un Évêque, après le Concordat.* Paris, Lecoffre, 1898.
CHAINE (LÉON). *Les Catholiques français et leurs difficultés actuelles.* Paris, Storck, 1903.

272 BIBLIOGRAPHY

CHAINE (LÉON). *Menus Propos d'un Catholique Libéral.* Paris, Nourry, 1908.

SABATIER (PAUL). *À propos de la Séparation des Églises et de l'État.* Paris, Fischbacher, 1905.

—— 2nd edition of same, enlarged. Paris, Fischbacher.

—— *Disestablishment in France* (English translation of above). Fisher Unwin, 1906.

—— *Lettre Ouverte à S.E. le Cardinal Gibbons à propos de son Manifeste sur la Séparation des Églises et de l'État en France.* Paris, Fischbacher, 1907.

RIFAUX (Dr. MARCEL). *Les Conditions du Retour au Catholicisme.* Paris, Plon-Nourrit, 1907.

KLEIN (l'Abbé FÉLIX). *Le Fait Religieux et la Manière de l'observer.* Paris, Lethielleux, 1903.

—— *Quelques motifs d'espérer.* Paris, Lecoffre, 1904.

—— *Au pays de "la Vie Intense."* Paris, Plon-Nourrit, 1904.

FOGAZZARO (ANTONIO). *Ascensioni Umani.* Milano. Baldini, 1899.

SEMERIA (GIOVANNI). *L'Eredità del Secolo.* Genova, Donatti, 1900.

—— *Le Vie della Fede.* Roma, Pustet, 1903.

—— *Scienza e Fede.* Roma. Pustet, 1903.

MINOCCHI (Prof. Salvatore). *La Crisi Odierna del Cattolicismo in Germania.* Firenze, Ariani. 1907.

GALLARATI-SCOTTI (Marchese TOMMASO). *Discorso Inaugurale del Primo Congresso della Lega Democratica Nazionale.* Milano, 1906.

Quello che Vogliamo. Lettera aperta di un gruppo di Sacerdoti (privately printed and circulated).

What we Want. (English translation of above.) Murray, 1907.

Il Programma dei Modernisti. Risposta all'Enciclica di Pio X, "Pascendi Dominici Gregis." Roma, Società Internazionale Scientifico-Religiosa Editrice, 1907.

The Programme of Modernism. (English translation of above.) Fisher Unwin, 1908.

(c) SOME WORKS OF TECHNICAL SCHOLARSHIP BY LEADING LIBERAL CATHOLIC SCHOLARS

LOISY (l'Abbé ALFRED). *Histoire du Canon de l'Ancien Testament.* Paris, Picard, 1890.

—— *Histoire du Canon du Nouveau Testament.* Paris, Picard, 1891.

—— *Études Bibliques.* Paris, Picard, 1901.

—— *Les Mythes Babyloniens et les premiers chapitres de la Genèse.* Paris, Picard, 1901.

LOISY *La Religion d'Israel.* Paris, Picard, 1901.
—— *Études Évangéliques.* Paris, Picard, 1902.
—— *Le Quatrième· Évangile.* Paris, Picard, 1903.
—— *Morceaux d'Exégèse.* Paris, Picard, 1906.
TURMEL (l'Abbé JOSEPH). *Histoire de la Théologie Positive depuis l'origine au Concile de Trente.* Paris, Beauchesne, 1904.
—— *Histoire de la Théologie Positive depuis le Concile de Trente au Concile du Vatican.* Paris, Beauchesne, 1907.
—— *Saint Jérôme.* Paris, Bloud, 1906.
—— *L'Eschatologie à la fin du IVe. Siècle,* extrait de la *Revue d'Histoire et de Littérature Religieuses,* Macon, 1900.
—— *Le Péché Originel après Saint Augustin.* (*La Revue d'Histoire et de Littérature Religieuses*), 1903 and 1904.
BATIFFOL (Mgr. PIERRE). *Études d'Histoire et de Théologie Positive.* 1ère série. Paris, Lecoffre, 1902.
—— —— 2me série. Paris, Lecoffre, 1905.
DUCHESNE (Mgr. LOUIS). *Fastes Épiscopaux de l'Ancienne Gaule.* 3 vols. Paris, Fontemoing, 1894.
—— *Églises Separées.* Paris, Fontemoing, 1896.
—— *Origines du Culte Chrétien.* Paris, Fontemoing, 1898.
—— *Christian Worship. Its Origin and Evolution.* (English translation of above.) C.K.S., 1903.
—— *Histoire Ancienne de l'Église.* Vol. 1. Paris, Fontemoing, 1906.
—— *Histoire Ancienne de l'Église.* Vol. II. Paris, Fontemoing, 1907.
VACANDARD (l'Abbé E.). *L'Inquisition et le Pouvoir Coercitif de l'Église.* Paris, Bloud, 1906.
DELEHAYE (le Père HIPPOLYTE, S. J.). *Les Légendes Hagiographiques.* Bruxelles, Société des Bollandistes, 1905.
—— *The Legends of the Saints.* (English translation of above.) KEGAN PAUL, 1907.
CHEVALIER (le Chanoine ULYSSE). *Notre Dame de Lorette.* Paris, Picard, 1906.
DUFOURCQ (ALBERT). *Étude sur les Gesta Martyrum.* Paris, Fontemoing, 1900.
TIXERONT (l'Abbé J.). *La Théologie Anténicéenne.* Paris, Lecoffre, 1905.
DUPIN (A.). *Le Dogme de la Trinité dans les trois premiers siècles.* Paris, Nourry, 1907.
HOUTIN (l'Abbé ALBERT.) *La Controverse de l'Apostolicité des Églises de France au XIXe. Siècle.* Paris, Fontemoing.
CALMES (le Père TH.). *L'Évangile Selon Saint Jean.* Paris, Lecoffre, 1904.

274 BIBLIOGRAPHY

LAGRANGE (le Père M. J.). *La Méthode Historique.* Paris, Lecoffre.
—— *Le Livre des Juges.* Paris, Lecoffre, 1903.
—— *Études sur les Religions Sémitiques.* Paris, Lecoffre, 1905.
GIGOT (Rev. FRANCIS E.). *General Introduction to the Study of the Holy Scriptures.* New York. Benzinger.
—— *Special Introduction to the Study of the Old Testament.* Part I, *The Historical Books.* New York, Benzinger.
—— —— Part II, *Didactic and Prophetical Books.* New York, Benzinger, 1906.
SCHELL (Dr. HERMANN). *Christus.* Mainz, Kirchheim, 1904.
KRAUS (Dr. F. Z.). *Cavour.* Mainz, Kirchheim, 1902.
—— *Essays.* 2 vols. Berlin, 1896.
—— *Dante, Sein Leben und Sein Werk.* Berlin, 1897.
EHRHARD (Dr. ALBERT). *Der Katholizismus und das Zwanzigste Jahrhundert.* Stuttgart & Wien, 1902.
—— *Liberaler Katholizismus?* Stuttgart & Wien, 1902.
ZAPLETAL (VINCENZ, O. P.). *Alttestamentliches.* Freiburg (Schweiz), 1903.
SEMERIA (GIOVANNI). *Dogma, Gerarchia, e Culto nella Chiesa Primitiva.* Roma, Pustet. 1902.
—— *Venticinque anni di Storia del Cristianesimo nascente.* Roma, Pustet, 1900.
—— *Il primo Sangue Cristiano.* Roma, Pustet, 1901.
—— *Il Pensiero di San Paolo nella Lettera ai Romani.* Roma, Pustet, 1903.
—— *La Messa nella sua Storia e nei suoi Simboli.* Roma, Pustet, 1904.
BUONAIUTI (Don ERNESTO). *Lo Gnosticismo.* Roma, Ferrari, 1907.
MINOCCHI (Prof. SALVATORE). *I Salmi tradotti dal testo originale e commentati.* Roma, Pustet, 1905.
—— *Storia dei Salmi e dell' Idea Messianica.* Roma, Pustet, 1902.
—— *Il Nuovo Testamento tradotto e annotato*—1. *I Vangeli.* Roma, Pustet, 1900.
—— *Le Profezie d'Isaia, tradotte e commentate.* Bologna, Matteuzzi, 1907.

Many important articles of both critical and general interest are also to be found in the *Revue d'Histoire et de Littérature Religieuses.* (1896-1907), the *Studi Religiosi* (1901-1907), and the *Annales de Philosophie Chrétienne.* The two former reviews ceased to exist with the end of the year 1907.

(This Bibliography makes no pretence to be exhaustive. It has been formed for the most part from works in my own possession, and the date given is occasionally, therefore, that of a second or later edition. In some cases I have not been able to trace the date of publication.)

INDEX OF NAMES

275